Conceptual Foundations of Language Science

No scientific work proceeds without conceptual foundations. In language science, our concepts about language determine our assumptions, direct our attention, and guide our hypotheses and our reasoning. Only with clarity about conceptual foundations can we pose coherent research questions, design critical experiments, and collect crucial data. This series publishes short and accessible books that explore well-defined topics in the conceptual foundations of language science. The series provides a venue for conceptual arguments and explorations that do not require the traditional book-length treatment, yet that demand more space than a typical journal article allows.

In this series:

1. Enfield, N. J. Natural causes of language.
2. Müller, Stefan. A lexicalist account of argument structure: Template-based phrasal LFG approaches and a lexical HPSG alternative.
3. Schmidtke-Bode, Karsten, Natalia Levshina, Susanne Maria Michaelis & Ilja A. Seržant (eds.). Explanation in typology: Diachronic sources, functional motivations and the nature of the evidence.
4. Morley, Rebecca L. Sound structure and sound change: A modeling approach.
5. Asoulin, Eran. Language and scientific explanation: Where does semantics fit in?
6. Boeckx, Cedric. Reflections on language evolution: From minimalism to pluralism.

ISSN: 2363-877X

Reflections on language evolution

From minimalism to pluralism

Cedric Boeckx

language
science
press

Cedric Boeckx. 2021. *Reflections on language evolution: From minimalism to pluralism* (Conceptual Foundations of Language Science 6). Berlin: Language Science Press.

This title can be downloaded at:
http://langsci-press.org/catalog/book/142

ISBN: 978-3-96110-328-7 (Digital)
978-3-98554-024-2 (Hardcover)

ISSN: 2363-877X
DOI: 10.5281/zenodo.5524633
Source code available from www.github.com/langsci/142
Collaborative reading: paperhive.org/documents/remote?type=langsci&id=142

Cover and concept of design: Ulrike Harbort
Proofreading: Jeroen van de Weijer, Lachlan Mackenzie
Fonts: Libertinus, Arimo, DejaVu Sans Mono
Typesetting software: XƎLATEX

Language Science Press
xHain
Grünberger Str. 16
10243 Berlin, Germany
langsci-press.org

Storage and cataloguing done by FU Berlin

Freie Universität Berlin

Contents

Acknowledgments

I am indebted to Mark Dingemanse for inviting me (several years ago) to contribute to the series he co-edits, and giving me the opportunity to support the *Language Science Press* initiative. I am grateful to Mark for commenting on earlier versions of the manuscript, and for not giving up on me as I was taking much longer than anticipated in wrapping up the manuscript.

The core ideas contained in this essay were presented in 2021 at the "Future of Linguistics" workshop organized by the Max Planck Institute for Psycholinguistics. I am very grateful to the directors of the Institute for inviting me to take part in this workshop, and (again) to Mark Dingemanse for seizing this opportunity to renew his invitation for me to write something for the *Conceptual Foundations of Language Science* series. Preparing for the "Future of Linguistics" lecture helped me enormously in organizing my thinking. Limor Raviv's input was also extremely valuable in bringing the essay to completion.

Although this is a short "book" ("pamphlet" would be a better term, I feel), many people contributed to the ideas I present in it. The book reflects the evolution of my own thinking on the language sciences and language evolution over the past decade, and there are many people to thank. Doing so properly would require a book of its own, so I will limit myself to listing key influences.

Articulating conceptual arguments is a bit like constructing an edifice. You need a firm foundation, help with the overall building design, a strong team to make it all happen, as well as constant attention to the surrounding area and ecosystem.

For providing me with a firm foundation, I am grateful to Noam Chomsky, Howard Lasnik, Juan Uriagereka, Alec Marantz, Ray Jackendoff, Norbert Hornstein, Jean-Roger Vergnaud, Marc Hauser, and Massimo Piattelli-Palmarini.

For making me think harder and better about the overall enterprise, I am extremely grateful to Simon Kirby, Simon Fisher, David Poeppel, and Dick Lewontin. I owe them a lot. Conversations with Gary Marcus, Gena Konopka, Tecumseh Fitch, Sonja Vernes, and Andrea Martin over the years were also extremely important in shaping my own thinking.

I have been extremely fortunate to receive the help of terrific students and collaborators, without whom I would be left with just empty promises. Thank you Constantina Theofanopoulou, Pedro Tiago Martins, Saleh Alamri, Bridget Samuels, Aritz Irurtzun, Rie Asano, Tom O'Rourke, Alejandro Andirko, Juan Moriano, Raul Buisan, Carmen Saldaña, Simone Gastaldon, Marcel Ruland, Sara Silvente, Ilaria Dutto, Giuseppe Testa and all the wonderful members of the Testa lab in Milan (which feels like a second home to me), Martin Kuhlwilm, Erich Jarvis, Bill Thompson, Bart de Boer, Andrea Ravignani, and the superb Evolinguistics community in Japan led by Kaz Okanoya and Koji Fujita. I have learned so much from each and everyone of them.

For making me appreciate more the richness and variety of approaches in the language sciences, and for providing, through her own work, a model for how to integrate them in an evolutionary context, I owe a special note of gratitude to Limor Raviv.

For supporting my group's work, I acknowledge support from the Spanish Ministry of Science and Innovation (grant PID2019-107042GB-I00), and from the Generalitat de Catalunya (2017-SGR-341).

I am grateful to Pedro Tiago Martins, Bridget Samuels and Rie Asano, trusted friends and former students, for taking the time to read and comment generously on a pre-final draft of this manuscript at short notice. Thank you also to Matt Spike and another, anonymous, reviewer for offering valuable suggestions. The book would be much better (but also much longer!) if I had been able to work them all into the final manuscript. Thanks also to Jeroen van de Weijer and Lachlan Mackenzie for proof-reading, and to Sebastian Nordhoff for assistance.

As my thinking evolved, two mentors (Morris Halle and Sylvain Bromberger) passed away. Like many others, I was extremely fortunate to learn from them and benefit from their advice. I am sorry Morris and Sylvain are no longer here for me to ask them questions and seek their wisdom, but some of the lessons they taught me remain very much with me.

1 Why (I) care about Darwin's Problem

This essay discusses in a somewhat informal way, with far too few references and well short of any adequate acknowledgements, what thinking about "Darwin's Problem"—the problem of language evolution—has taught me about the nature of language and the landscape of the language sciences.[1]

I like the term "Darwin's Problem" as a way to refer to the problem of human language evolution, because it echoes the nomenclature introduced in Chomsky 1986, to talk about the logical problems of language acquisition ("Plato's Problem"), language knowledge ("Humboldt's Problem") and use ("Descartes' Problem"). The term "Darwin's Problem" makes clear that this evolutionary focus is part of a family of questions that constitutes a research program very much in line with Tinbergen's "Four Questions" program for ethology, which integrates mechanism, function, ontogeny, and phylogeny (Tinbergen 1963). Indeed, different approaches to Darwin's problem often go hand in hand with specific approaches to other issues such as language acquisition.[2]

Although other questions have occupied pride of place in linguistics, Darwin's Problem is my favorite, not only because I'd love to know how the modern human language faculty came to be, but also, and perhaps more importantly, because methodologically speaking it is the question that unambiguously makes the language sciences part of the biological sciences. Studying human language means different things to different people, and that's perfectly legitimate. A focus on the underlying biology is by no means the only option. I got into linguistics

[1] An important caveat: The reflections that follow are necessarily biased by lots of factors, not least of which is my professional training in a particular linguistic/cognitive tradition. I apologize if at times this professional deformation leads me to use a generic term like "linguistics" when sometimes I means "the particular type of linguistic tradition I grew up in" (for background, see my own work: Boeckx 2006, 2009, as well as the thoughtful reflections in Marantz 2019). While I am fully aware of the severe limitations of this characterization, readers familiar with other linguistic frameworks should not feel alienated. I am only using the generative tradition as a foil, and advocate a far more inclusive vision for the language sciences in this essay.

[2] To give one example, I don't think that the difficulties faced by the standard generative treatment in the context of Darwin's problem are totally independent of the difficulties the standard generative treatment faces in the context of language acquisition. A much more comprehensive essay than the one I am able to offer here is required to articulate such interdependencies.

not because of an inordinate love for languages, but because of the promise (going all the way back to Descartes, and likely even earlier philosophers, Chomsky 1966) that understanding this capacity that we have to develop at least one language is bound to tell us something deep about who we are. That's a humanities question alright, but everybody's guess is that the answer is ultimately rooted in biology; and this means, in light of Dobzhansky's famous dictum ("Nothing makes sense in biology except in the light of evolution", Dobzhansky 1973), evolutionary biology. Chomsky's frequent point (see, e.g., Chomsky 2012) that even when placed in the same environment, only a child, but not a kitten or a rock, ends up acquiring a language is deep down about Darwin's Problem: it compares creatures and points to the species-specific character of the trait in question. It's the quintessential question of what makes (made) us human.

Of all the Tinbergian questions on the agenda of the language sciences, Darwin's Problem is the most interdisciplinary one of all. You can't investigate it in the privacy of your linguistics office. That is unlike, say, the problem of what knowledge of language is. For the latter, linguists have (successfully) proceeded pretty much like philologists did in the past: analyzing (parts of) sentences, across languages. Familiar data, modulo the odd sentence construction. You can't (seriously) do this in the context of Darwin's Problem. I know some people have tried: they have looked for "fossils" – modern language constructions that (they claim) linguistic theory would single out as "simpler"; and interpreted these essentially as relics or vestiges of a simpler, pre-linguistic/proto-linguistic system. Bickerton 1984, Jackendoff 1999, and, in a book-length format, Progovac 2015 are among those who have advocated this approach. I have written about why I find this non-compelling (Boeckx 2016). At the end of the day, these "fossils" are modern language constructions, and their proto-linguistic status rests on some speculation about what proto-language was (as well as on the researchers' analytic biases regarding what counts as "simple constructions"). But how do we know? Indeed, how could we possibly know in the absence of linguistic documents from that long-gone era?

This *modus operandi* is very different from the approach pioneered in Kirby 2001, and now pursued by many researchers: the iterated learning paradigm looks at language(-like) data (artificial grammars), and tests participants that have a modern language capacity, but the goal is to distill generic biases that drive the learning process (and the results are crucially validated in computational models where biases can be controlled for). Unlike the search for language fossils, the iterated learning paradigm can be readily exported to other domains, and indeed the iterated learning paradigm has been applied to non-language material (whistles, drawings, etc.) (Cornish et al. 2013, Verhoef et al. 2013). The language(-like) data is not essential to the iterated learning paradigm. But it is essential for the fossilized-construction studies (which invariably rely on jargon that is not free from theoretical dispute). In the latter case philologists/traditional grammarians feel at home. In the former, maybe less so.

The iterated learning paradigm is just one of the many ways in which Darwin's Problem has become empirically tractable, "experimentable" in the lab. Progress in genetics offers other experimental opportunities. Refined methods in comparative psychology offer yet others. All of these options are now open to language scientists. But they won't attract the linguists only at ease amidst (parts of) sentences. That's the great value of thinking about Darwin's Problem: it forces you to make a choice: which draws you more? The nature of language data, or the nature of cognition? Do you take language to be the ultimate goal, or the means to get there? If you have to make constructive comparisons with species that don't have language, the answer is inescapable.

Darwin's Problem is also great at forcing linguists to be specific about what Gallistel called "the foundational abstractions" (Gallistel 2009). Along with Krakauer et al. 2017, I agree that the cognitive descriptions of behavior have a lot to contribute to work in other disciplines. But we can't just ask the folks across the border to read our textbooks. The textbooks train their readers in a particular discipline. We must get these texts down to basics; stick to the essentials. Ideally, frame these in generic terms; otherwise, they won't "get past customs", as it were. This is a massive "mapping" problem, as David Poeppel has called it (Poeppel 2012), expanding on the important reflections in Poeppel & Embick 2005. It is of the utmost importance. For language, I side with Fitch 2014 and Uriagereka 2008, and think that some of the earliest descriptions of linguistic computations, such as some of those found in Chomsky 1957 and reviewed in the first chapters of Lasnik 2000, constitute a rock-solid foundation. Notice that in those early studies, actual (parts of) sentences played no role. It was all algebraic: terminal symbols, non-terminal symbols, transformations, monostrings, etc.[3] I find this ideally suited for fruitful comparisons with species that don't manipulate (parts of) sentences of the familiar sort.

Of course, some might say this is not "core" linguistics. That's fine. Language is such a rich and complex phenomenon that different people are entitled to differ-

[3]Indeed, on the first page of Chomsky 1957 one reads: "The ultimate outcome of these investigations should be a theory of linguistic structure in which the descriptive devices utilized in particular grammars are presented and studied abstractly, with no specific reference to particular languages." I do not think that Chomsky's statement is an encouragement to ignore data from languages, but rather (and more interestingly) an invitation to develop a linguistic theory that remains useful even when traditional data points are not available.

ent opinions about language. What's clear in the context of Darwin's Problem is that language is not a thing. It is many things put together: it's a mosaic, a patchwork, a complex system – a conjunction of many parts that have come together in the course of evolution. Linguists would call it a compound.

Interestingly, linguists distinguish between two types of compound. There are compounds like *handbag*, where one of the parts is clearly dominant (a handbag is a bag, not a hand). Such compounds are called endocentric. There are other compounds, like *football* (the game), that are called exocentric, where all the parts are equally important. In light of Hauser et al. 2002, one could say that linguists tend to think of the human faculty of language as an endocentric compound. Sure, they say, the language faculty consists of many parts, but some parts are more important than others. These would constitute the core, and the rest would be "externalized" to the periphery. The bet here is that the core is species-unique. I think this renders cross-species comparison particularly difficult. It's too easy to turn the core of the compound into a mountain that is too tall to climb for other species. It leads to a kind of exceptional nativism—something irreducibly unique about human language. Comparative psychology becomes necessarily contrastive. The alternative, which I favor, is one that takes the language faculty to be akin to an exocentric compound: all parts are needed to make a unique whole, but none of the parts, on their own, are unique. As such, it's just a matter of identifying them, across cognitive domains, scattered among organisms. I think that's the only way to climb "mount improbable", to use Richard Dawkins' apt phrase.

The leitmotivs that animate and structure this essay are thus:

(i) renewed appreciation for the comparative method applied to cognitive questions, leading to the identification of elementary but fundamental abstractions in non-linguistic species relevant to language

(ii) awareness of the conceptual gaps between disciplines, and the need to carefully link genotype and phenotype without bypassing any "intermediate" levels of description (certainly not the brain)

(iii) adoption of a "philosophical" outlook that puts the complexity of biological entities front and center

I see these three themes as the ingredients of the current zeitgeist, which is aimed at reducing distance between species and levels of analysis. Hopefully, the discussion that follows will encourage linguists to take part in this interdisciplinary enterprise.

At the end of the day, Darwin's Problem is a question that opens the field of language studies like no other I know of. That's why I agree with Steve Levinson's assertion that "real progress is likely to come from an evolutionary perspective".[4] Darwin's problem is the only one that has made me revise my understanding of language based on progress in other fields; progress that seems so fundamental that it requires a shift of perspective in order to be integrated (the *FOXP2* literature being a prime example; Fisher 2019). It's the only one that expanded my data set (filling it with data of different kinds, from different species, from birds to bats to baboons). It's the only question that has left me without any excuse for not doing biology.

[4]https://www.mpi.nl/imprs100/the-germ-of-an-idea

2 An evolving landscape

Around a decade ago, an important review article entitled "Language evolution in the laboratory" (Scott-Phillips & Kirby 2010) was published in *Trends in Cognitive Sciences*. Its central message, in my opinion, was that it was becoming possible, at last, to approach at least certain aspects of language evolution in a scientific manner. This was a sharp departure from over a century of statements declaring that language evolution was a mystery.

Remnants of this old attitude still exist (Hauser et al. 2014); they typically invoke in a tedious fashion the 1866 ban on all discussion of the evolution of language imposed by the Linguistic Society of Paris; they also frequently cite Lewontin's pronouncement that we will never know why cognition evolved the way it did (Lewontin 1998). But things have changed quite dramatically over the past two decades, so much so that it has become possible to contemplate "controlled hypothesis-testing through experimentation" (Motamedi et al. 2019) in the domain of language evolution.

I still recall being told as a graduate student that the topic of language evolution was more a matter of science fiction than science, and that this was best left as a domain of study for after retirement. Today, some of the brightest students I know are actively engaged in this field, illustrating the massive progress made over the past 20 years, well attested in the Proceedings of the Evolang conference series, as well as in the creation of centers for the study of language evolution in Edinburgh and more recently Z'urich. The main change (still ongoing), to my mind, is the resistance to exploring hypotheses until they can be formulated in a way that can be put to the test. A change from 'I think *x*' to 'I think *x* and I can test *x* doing *y*.'

The efforts of members of the Centre for Language Evolution at the University of Edinburgh, led by Simon Kirby, have shown how combining the development of artificial languages (mini-grammars) in a laboratory setting (Kirby et al. 2008, 2015), as well as agent-based modelling approaches controlling for biases that language users in the lab bring to the task in an unconscious manner (Thompson et al. 2016), reveals how learnability and expressivity pressures shape grammars. Subsequent work from other centers (e.g. Raviv et al. 2019, Raviv 2020, Raviv et al. 2021) also experimentally demonstrates how communicative contexts impact grammar formation and the emergence of new languages. While it is often said that such work only addresses language change ('glossogeny'), and not language evolution proper (language phylogeny, the emergence of the modern language capacity),[1] I do not find this dichotomy particularly useful, and believe that a continuum of cognitive biases that interact with changing communicative conditions from which language-readiness emerges, shaping the range of grammars acquired, is a more adequate stance (more on this in chapter 4).

The same year the review article by Scott-Phillips & Kirby 2010 appeared, the first draft of the Neanderthal genome was published (Green et al. 2010), starting a revolution that continues unabated to this day (Reich 2018). As we will see later on, the successful retrieval of ancient DNA, from a few skeletal remains and now even cave sediments, and of ancient proteins, allows us to ask questions at an unprecedented level of resolution and dramatically changes what we mean by "fossil record". The debt we owe to Svante Pääbo and his collaborators is hard to overstate (Pääbo 2014a, Meyer et al. 2012, Prüfer et al. 2014, 2017, Mafessoni et al. 2020, Slon et al. 2017, Vernot et al. 2021, Zavala et al. 2021, Welker et al. 2016, 2020).

Yet this massive amount of data that is now accessible would be "empty" if it were not for the progress made in linking the genotype and the phenotype. In the domain of language, the work pioneered by Simon Fisher on *FOXP2* is the gold standard (Lai et al. 2001), and arguably one of the most significant achievements in the language sciences in the past twenty five years (Fisher & Scharff 2009, Fisher & Vernes 2015, Fisher 2019, Den Hoed et al. 2021). It has taught us that for all the intricacies and levels of analyses separating genes and behavior, careful work can illuminate central issues that Lenneberg could only dream of when he wrote his classic book, *Biological Foundations of Language*, over fifty years ago (Lenneberg 1967).

Equally important for the success of what is sometimes called "evolinguistics" is the dramatic shift of perspective that took place in the domain of comparative psychology. This is well-captured in the following passage from de Waal & Ferrari 2010:

> Over the last few decades, comparative cognitive research has focused on the pinnacles of mental evolution, asking all-or-nothing questions such as which animals (if any) possess a theory of mind, culture, linguistic abilities, future planning, and so on. Research programs adopting this top-down perspective have often pitted one taxon against another, resulting in sharp dividing lines. Insight into the underlying mechanisms has lagged behind …

[1]Terminology introduced in Hurford 1990.

> A dramatic change in focus now seems to be under way, however, with increased appreciation that the basic building blocks of cognition might be shared across a wide range of species. We argue that this bottom-up perspective, which focuses on the constituent capacities underlying larger cognitive phenomena, is more in line with both neuroscience and evolutionary biology.

In the domain of language, calls for recognizing an ever broader "community of descent", to borrow a phrase from Darwin 1871, are more and more frequent (Lattenkamp & Vernes 2018). Far from being rhetorical, these calls demonstrate how much one can learn about our kind by studying behavior in numerous species in accordance with Tinbergen's multi-level approach.

As Ernst Mayr was fond of saying, "evolutionary biology [unlike physics] is a historical science, [where] one constructs a historical narrative, consisting of a tentative reconstruction of the particular scenario that led to the events one is trying to explain" (Mayr 2000). Narratives will continue to dominate evolutionary investigations into language, but crucially, thanks to the progress made in key areas that I singled out above, these narratives are enriched with, and constrained by, "numbers". Hypotheses can now be put to the test.

It becomes very apparent in this context that simple narratives, appealing as they may appear, are hopelessly misguided. Recalling the words of H. L. Mencken, "For every complex problem there is an answer that is clear, simple, and wrong". What more complex problem is there than the problem of language evolution?

Accordingly, the simple, clear, "minimalist", and influential evolutionary scenario advocated by Berwick and Chomsky in their book *Why Only Us* (Berwick & Chomsky 2016) must be wrong.[2] I have tried to say so on several occasions (Boeckx 2017, Martins & Boeckx 2019, de Boer et al. 2020). Very briefly: it is wrong because it disregards the comparative evidence ('only us'), it fails to appreciate the multi-level approach required to link genotype and phenotype (claiming that a single mutation yields the simple, atomic operation "merge"), it keeps the discussion at the logical level, without attempting to even sketch a plausible path to testing it, and does not engage with the many lessons coming from the great discoveries in paleo-sciences over the past decade.

The reason I have spent time arguing against Berwick and Chomsky's narrative is not only because it was proposed by influential linguists, but because it

[2] If I am right, this has non-trivial ramifications for the minimalist program. Over the years, talk of optimization, efficiency, etc., which occupied center stage in the early days of the program, has been replaced by a focus on evolutionary considerations. If such considerations lead to an impasse, the program as a whole may indeed have been (at best) premature.

is representative of a family of approaches that linguists remain attracted to: it presupposes that other animals don't have much to teach us about the core of our language faculty, because essentially they are non-linguistic creatures. The gap between them and us is a chasm. It also takes for granted that our language capacity is very recent in evolutionary terms, going back maybe 150 000 years. As such, so the claim goes, there was very little time to evolve a "kludgy" language organ (cf. Marcus 2009). Accordingly, a narrative must be developed that keeps the core language faculty essentially free of evolutionary tinkering.

Such a narrative (in many ways, the culmination of the minimalist program envisaged by Chomsky) clashes with recent attempts to attribute a significant portion of our "modern" language faculty to the last common ancestor shared with our closest extinct relatives (Dediu & Levinson 2013, 2018). It also clashes with mounting evidence for a complex, temporally very extended, mosaic-like evolution of our lineage (Scerri et al. 2018, Bergström et al. 2021). Also, it makes certain assumptions about how many changes can be favored by natural selection within a relatively short window of time which are not obviously true—indeed, very implausible (de Boer et al. 2020). Last, but not least, it grants too much power to linguistic theorizing. As argued in Martins & Boeckx 2019, it is fallacious to draw a direct correspondence between the formal structure of a computational operation and the biological changes that would lead to it.[3] It is what theoretical linguists would love to be able to do: it would make their theoretical work immediately relevant for evolutionary claims. But it is logically incorrect. This is precisely why, in my opinion, evolutionary considerations impact how we do theoretical linguistics, or how we see the import of that work. If there is no such direct correspondence, if the link between genotype and phenotype is very complex indeed, I do not see any alternative to painstakingly developing linking hypotheses that, we hope, progressively spell out what it means to say that our linguistic condition is part of our human (biological) condition.

I want to insist once more on the importance of debunking simple accounts like Berwick and Chomsky's. It may well be that there will be certain behaviors or artifacts or anatomical traits that we can confidently ascribe exclusively to members of our species that "emerged" recently. Right now this is being questioned, but I would not be surprised if we are left with a small set of recent "*sapiens*-exclusive" properties (brain changes giving rise to our globular skull, use of complex symbiotic tools like the bow and arrow, and some aspects of figurative art are fairly good bets in my current opinion), but crucially, even if the evidence

[3]In their reply to Martins & Boeckx 2019, Berwick & Chomsky 2019 completely—and surprisingly—miss this point; see Martins & Boeckx 2020a for illustration.

settles along these lines, it should not be used to argue for a recent cognitive revolution that matches a minimalist vision of the language faculty. Rather, such evidence will have to be integrated into the complex mosaic of language that evolution has constructed over an extended period of time.

This is certainly a major lesson I learned from thinking about Darwin's problem: Evolutionary considerations invalidate certain theoretical frameworks that fail to come to grips with the "complex dynamical system" nature of language. The next two chapters deal with other lessons that pertain to a broader range of approaches, and implicate a larger number of researchers: even those linguists that readily accept that the evolutionary trajectory of our language capacity was long and complex still subscribe to certain views that I think we would do well to abandon. I'll focus on three such views here. One is that somehow, there is at least one aspect of language (typically, some aspect of syntax) that makes our language capacity special, and that as a result forms some sort of barrier in a comparative setting. Another is the belief that linguistic theory matters and that one's theory of language evolution depends on one's theory of language. And third, the claim that because languages don't leave fossils, the evidence for studying the evolution of language is too sparse. These three claims are incorrect.

3 Lessons we still have to learn

I do not want to fall into the temptation of considering a field like theoretical linguistics that has traditionally focused on the (cognitive) phenotype as "quaint, old-fashioned, or incapable of deep insight". I borrow this phrase from Jarrett & Kilner 2018, who use it to say that now that we are living in the Age of the Genome, it is all too easy to characterize in this (negative) way fields of biological research that analyze the phenotype. Although I have come to question many assumptions made in the linguistic tradition I grew up in, I think there is a lot of value to that work, and lots of insights worth integrating.[1]

Here is a key result worth preserving: the attention to what Marr 1982 called the "computational" level, and in particular, the type of formal characterization that was at the center of the earliest work in generative grammar, and that gave rise to what is informally known as the "Chomsky hierarchy" of formal languages, now perhaps more familiar to students in computer science than in linguistics. Chomsky 1956, 1957 demonstrated that words in natural languages are not arranged like beads on a string, and from there went on to discuss the relevance of considerations pertaining to "context-free" and "context-sensitive" grammars and associated memory structures to capture patterns of dependencies attested in language (for a detailed and accessible retelling of these central arguments, see Lasnik 2000).[2] I agree with O'Donnell et al. 2005, Fitch 2014 that this early work contains deep, long-lasting results, with the additional advantage of being "theory-free" in the sense that (unlike more recent results) it does not

[1]Most of the problems I use here as illustrations are drawn from the realm of syntax. I do so largely because this has traditionally been the domain over which species-specificity has been defined, especially in the linguistics tradition I am most familiar with. This is not to say that this is the only interesting area of research. Semantics and pragmatics are other domains of great relevance, but here I feel significant progress has already been made, pointing to substantial evolutionary continuity. I personally found the treatments in Hurford 2007, Moore 2018a,b, Krupenye & Call 2019 very compelling.

[2]Without getting into technicalities of formal language theory, I take it to be absolutely essential to recognize the need for dependencies that go beyond the range of adjacent elements, and recognize hierarchically organized expressions forming both nested and crossing dependencies; that is, dependencies of the "if …then" sort, and those dependencies underlying the organization of the English verbal complex (see Lasnik 2000 for extensive discussion): *John and Sally (may) (have) (been) run(ning).*

depend on any "technical" intricacy or jargon that is peculiar to a particular linguistic framework or tradition.[3] As such, these are results that have the potential to translate more easily across fields, and can readily inform research beyond the narrow confines of linguistics departments.

As a matter of fact, Chomsky's early characterization of linguistic rules and representations, refined over the years, in particular thanks to the insights of Aravind Joshi (Joshi 1985), constitutes an under-appreciated "consensus" that Ed Stabler has done well to highlight in recent years (Stabler 2011, 2013). As Stabler states, over the years a "substantial, non-trivial consensus about the nature of linguistic structure has emerged" over a wide range of theoretical approaches. Though often hidden behind jargon, numerous independently-proposed grammar formalisms (Stabler lists at least six of them) converge on a claim that goes back to Joshi 1985: natural languages are both strongly and weakly mildly context-sensitive. That is to say, mildly context-sensitive grammars "can both define the sentences of human languages (weak adequacy) and also provide the structures of those languages (strong adequacy)". To put it in other words, the range of dependencies that are attested in natural languages is constrained in a way that, following Chomsky's early description in *Syntactic Structures*, requires computational "power" (specific memory structures/representations) beyond the scope of finite-state automata and also beyond that of a class of "push-down automata" (associated with "context-free" grammars).

3.1 Choosing among grammar formalisms

This foundational result, whose robustness Stabler is right to emphasize, allows me to question a well-known statement made by Ray Jackendoff to the effect that "one's theory of language evolution depends on one's theory of language" (Jackendoff 2010). At first sight, Jackendoff's statement sounds like a truism, and as such is uncontroversial (in the same way, one would think, that one's view of language depends on one's view of evolution). But hidden behind this statement is a presupposition that the well-known and much-advertized fragmentation of the field of theoretical linguistics into fiercely contested traditions is highly relevant for thinking about Darwin's problem. In other words, it is claimed that one must choose one's theoretical allegiance carefully because doing so makes

[3] As a reviewer points out, this is not to say that the Chomsky hierarchy is the only game in town and free of problems (for useful discussion, see Rogers & Pullum 2011). My point here is a modest one: the Chomsky hierarchy is a useful tool to express explicitly essential points of convergence across linguistic frameworks.

quite different predictions about the evolutionary narrative one will tell. I think this is a massive overstatement. I am not questioning that different theoretical frameworks make different predictions about specific language data, but I am not convinced they make radically different testable predictions about evolutionary questions (more concerned with general "design features" of language, following Hockett's influential guidelines; Hockett 1960). As Stabler stresses, many grammar formalisms converge (unfortunately, in a "hidden", tacit fashion) on an abstract, computational characterization of human languages, and it is ultimately that point of convergence, that "epicenter of linguistic behavior", as Stabler 2013 calls it, borrowing a phrase by Tom Bever, that we want to ask evolutionary questions about. Put differently, there may well be far less disagreement about one's theory of language, and as such far more consensus about what it is that is to be captured when one theorizes about language evolution.

In particular, I think it is critical to realize that many linguists' theoretical considerations (what is the "right" analysis for indirect questions, or interjections, or infixation, etc.) do not bear on answerable evolutionary questions. I doubt we will ever be in a position to reconstruct with any certainty the specific grammatical constructions attested at a particular stage of, say, proto-language. In the absence of actual data, this strikes me as hopeless, as Lewontin 1998 would say. Instead, the focus should be on the range of grammatical constructions made possible at various stages of evolution, and there, Stabler's hidden consensus is extremely relevant.

What I think is needed to inform one's theory of language evolution is less focus on one's theory of language (where we can rely on the hidden consensus), and far more focus on how one's theory of language is integrated with other levels of analysis linking the genotype and the (computational/behavioral) phenotype: the neural predictions one's theory of language makes are of far greater importance for one's theory of language evolution. And here too, contrary to what Jackendoff's statement under discussion may suggest, there are far fewer options available than one might think; in this case, because few theoretical linguists engage with the interdisciplinary task of constructing linking hypotheses across levels of analysis, keeping the notorious slash between mind and brain, and hiding behind statements like "we know so little/nothing about the brain". Accordingly, I suggest we rephrase Jackendoff's statement as follows: One's theory of language evolution depends on one's linking hypotheses across levels of analysis.

This way of phrasing things has the advantage of bringing into focus a vitally important task for linguists and non-linguists alike: the importance of bridging the gap between mind and brain. I indeed believe that the strength of one's evolutionary narrative depends on how often the brain is alluded to in it (hence my preference for the use of the term "language-ready *brain*"). This is most clearly the case when one tries to exploit the expanding dataset generated by paleogeneticists: this is a fantastically rich resource of new data for linguists and cognitive scientists, but one that is silent about cognitive issues in the absence of well-articulated, patiently developed, experimentally tested conjunctions of hypotheses from genes to proteins to cells to circuits, the dynamics of these neural circuits and eventually to cognitive processes and representations. It is in this context that the insistence on tackling the "mapping problem" (Fisher 2014, Poeppel 2012) across all these levels is most acute. As correctly stated in Hagoort 2018, there is a prerequisite that must be fulfilled in order to present a solid evolutionary narrative on the human language-ready brain: one must first be explicit about the neurobiology at stake.

This, of course, does not mean that we have to understand everything about "language in the brain" ("Broca's problem", as one might call it) before embarking on Darwin's problem. Inquiry can proceed in parallel (I think it must, for evolutionary considerations will inform neurolinguistics), but neurobiological considerations have epistemological priority for the same reason Humboldt's problem ('what is knowledge of language?') has priority over the ultimately more fundamental problem of language acquisition (Plato's problem), as Chomsky already made clear in his review of Skinner's book *Verbal Behavior* (Chomsky 1959) and again in Chomsky 1986.

Incidentally, the very same detailed mapping between mind and brain is also clearly needed to address Darwin's problem's close cousin: Plato's problem. As developmental psycholinguist Evan Kidd put it in the context of language acquisition research,[4] "the frontier of the field will be the integration of neuroscience because, ultimately, it is our brains that are learning language. Understanding that process may well bring us closer to more psychologically plausible theories of how language is not only learned but also represented in the brain".

Tinbergen would be pleased to see how the strength of the field of cognitive biology of language depends on how answers to all his "why-questions" are integrated.

[4]https://knowablemagazine.org/article/mind/2020/how-babies-learn-language

3.2 How to think about evolutionary novelties

Apart from learning to work across levels of analysis and explanatory dimensions, there is a second lesson I think researchers in language evolution need to assimilate. It pertains to what we take to be "novel" or "special" about human language.

I will organize the discussion in this section around quotes from an influential paper that contributed to the revival of evolutionary considerations in some corners of linguistics, and that is concerned with the notion of evolutionary novelty (Hauser et al. 2002).[5]

As is well-known, Hauser et al. 2002 introduced a distinction between the Faculty of Language in the Broad Sense (FLB) and the Faculty of Language in the Narrow Sense (FLN) to invite "[l]inguists and biologists, along with researchers in the relevant branches of psychology and anthropology, [to] move beyond unproductive theoretical debate to a more collaborative, empirically focused and comparative research program". At bottom, the authors issue a renewed call for a robust comparative basis to study human cognition. They focus on the number of properties (traits, mechanisms, etc.) that human language shares with what can be found in other species, and designate these properties as "FLB". But they stress that "[s]omething about the faculty of language must be unique in order to explain the differences between humans and the other animals", which they label as "FLN".

Thanks to the emergence of compelling cases for deep homology (e.g., the convergence found among vocal learning animals (e.g., Pfenning et al. 2014), I sense that linguists are now quite comfortable with the claim that some aspects of our linguistic capacity are shared with other species. But although FLB was introduced to facilitate "productive discussion of language evolution", the whole FLB/FLN distinction may not have been the most felicitous way of redirecting attention to the need for a comparative, as opposed to a contrastive, approach to the study of human language evolution. The reason for this is the way the FLB/FLN discussion was framed: it may have helped perpetuate the idea that next to shared aspects (FLB), there are properties of our language faculty that are "special", "unique", or "species-specific" (FLN).

As Jackendoff & Pinker 2005 were quick to point out, "the Narrow/Broad dichotomy...makes space only for completely novel capacities and for capacities taken intact from nonlinguistic and nonhuman capacities, omitting capacities

[5] I am here drawing on ideas and selected quotes from Hauser et al. 2002 that I first discussed in Boeckx 2013. While the main message may not be news to biologists, I feel it is one that many linguists still need to assimilate. For a complementary perspective, see Fujita 2016.

that may have been substantially modified in the course of human evolution". The dichotomous way of framing the question using terms like FLN or FLB makes it hard to explore the many capacities that were gradually and substantially modified in the course of human evolution. Are these to be included in FLB or in FLN? Take the contribution of the much-discussed *FOXP2* gene in the context of language. While highly conserved across species, the gene is known to harbor two key mutations that are not found in our closest living relatives (chimpanzees) (Enard et al. 2002). Say, for the sake of the argument, that we succeed in establishing that these mutations contributed to our linguistic phenotype (not implausible in light of Enard et al. 2009). Would this be about FLB, or FLN? FLN, it seems to me, but not necessarily according to Hauser, Chomsky, and Fitch, who take the highly conserved nature of the gene to automatically make it part of FLB (Fitch et al. 2005).

At the heart of the FLN/FLB distinction is the attempt on the part of Hauser, Chomsky, and Fitch to grapple with the problem of innovation and novelty in biology. While biologists have made great progress over the past century and a half in understanding how existing traits diversify, much more modest progress has been made in understanding how novel traits come into being in the first place. To remedy this explanatory deficit, some biologists have first attempted to define what counts as a novelty (see, e.g., Müller & Newman 2005). In this context, it is worth noting the similarity between how Fitch et al. 2005 define FLN ("that which is specific to language and unique to humans") with the definition put forth in Müller & Wagner 1991: "a structure that is neither homologous to any structure in the ancestral species nor homologous to any other structure of the same organism".

When one turns to the relevant biology literature, one finds a consensus regarding how such novel structures arise (Moczek 2008, Linz et al. 2019, Prud'homme et al. 2011): phenotypic novelty is largely reorganizational. In other words, novelty arises from the combination of generic mechanisms, whose collective effects give rise to what appears to be *de novo* characters.

Interestingly, the possibility of emergent novelty is alluded to in Fitch et al. 2005: "Something about the faculty of language must be unique in order to explain the differences between humans and the other animals – if only the particular combination of mechanisms in FLB". But this seems to me to put in jeopardy the very FLN/FLB distinction.

The possibility of emergent, reorganizational novelty is present in some of Chomsky's own works (Chomsky 1978, 2000, 2004), but is always put into question as soon as it is considered.[6] Consider this quote from Chomsky 1978: "Now a question that could be asked is whether whatever is innate about language is specific to the language faculty or whether it is just some combination of the other aspects of the mind. That is an empirical question and there is no reason to be dogmatic about it; you look and you see. What we seem to find is that it is specific." This is unfortunate, for Chomsky's stance (which essentially boils down to the way in which the FLN/FLB distinction has been understood) indeed "mak[es] some hypotheses – in our view the most plausible ones – impossible to state" (Jackendoff & Pinker 2005): the FLN/FLB distinction, which is designed to separate the old from the new, focuses on component parts, and as such makes it difficult to understand the new as a collection of the old (the system as a whole). Perhaps for this reason, one finds in Fitch's more recent writings passages like this: "What all of these examples make clear is that the distinction between general and linguistically specialized mechanisms is hard to draw, even in those cases where the mechanisms themselves seem fairly clearly defined. Most areas of language are not, and will not soon be, so clearly defined, and thus the distinction itself is of little use in furthering our understanding of the mechanisms" (Fitch 2011).

I take Fitch's statement to mean that the FLN/FLB distinction, in the hands of linguists, turned out not to be so useful after all. I side with Bloomfield et al. 2011, according to whom, "[p]erhaps this is a good time to reconsider whether attempting to distinguish between qualitative and quantitative differences is helpful if the quantitative advantage is vast."

It is indeed puzzling that so many researchers still cling to the FLN/FLB distinction when the rationale behind the distinction given at the outset of Hauser et al. 2002 is to reject the notion of the faculty of language as a monolithic object: how can we identify if some mechanism is "specific to languagc" if "language" itself is not a well-defined, unique object?[7]

As discussed in Theofanopoulou & Boeckx 2015 the problematic nature of the FLN/FLB distinction is actually part of a larger problem concerning the construction of cognitive phylogenies (see also Martins & Boeckx 2020b). Although motivated by evolutionary considerations and an attempt to identify shared characteristics, accounts like Fitch et al. 2010 reveal assumptions that are at odds with the

[6] I agree with a reviewer that the dismissal of this emergentist possibility is not unrelated to the failure on the part of many linguists to appreciate the structuring role of "developmental noise". For relevant discussion, see Lewontin 2001, Mitchell 2018.

[7] Perhaps it is for this reason that the phrase "unique/specific to language" does not appear in the original 2002 paper, but only in Fitch et al. 2005 who take it from Pinker & Jackendoff 2005, where FLN is characterized in those terms for the first time (contrary to the literature that routinely attributes it to Hauser et al. 2002).

"entangled" nature of evolutionary products. Trying to map cognitive traits onto cladograms is treating these traits as encapsulated (Fodorian) modules (Fodor 1983), which they are clearly not. Defined as modules, cognitive traits retain a certain contrastive character: the defining feature of x (a species/cognitive trait) will be what is not shared. But what makes traits distinct, or species-specific, is the way their ingredients have come together in the course of evolution. The fascination with "brand-new properties" is largely due to the almost exclusive focus on the phenotypic level. But as soon as one asks how that phenotypic trait is implemented in the brain, how the neural circuit responsible for it is genetically encoded, one runs into the tinkering nature of evolution, and the massively generic nature of elementary operations below the phenotypic level.

Alternative approaches, such as the concept of reconstructing the evolutionary trajectory of behavior in terms of "phylogenetic refinement" (Cisek 2019), focused on neurophysiological mechanisms rather than "definitions of putative functions inherited from psychological traditions", strike me as far more productive. Certainly, the preceding paragraphs help cast further doubts on narratives focused on "component parts", like Berwick and Chomsky's about a syntactic operation like "Merge" being *the* basic property that adds content to FLN (Berwick & Chomsky 2016).

3.3 More continuity

To conclude this chapter, I present an argument for looking for pervasive continuity for each and every aspect of the human language faculty.

The case study I will sketch in this section is rooted in a long-standing idea within generative linguistics, and has even featured in a *Science* article (Heinz & Idsardi 2011). It is the idea that phonology and syntax (or sound patterns and sentence patterns) are quite different (Bromberger & Halle 1989); specifically, it is about the claim that human syntax requires more powerful computational resources, not attested in other species. An aspect of this idea has been used productively to argue for what Fitch 2018b has called "phonological continuity" across species—a hypothesis that goes back to Samuels 2011, 2015, where a compelling case for the presence of virtually all basic ingredients of human phonological rules and representations in non-linguistic creatures is presented.

The case for continuity in phonology exploits the well-established idea that, computationally speaking, phonological processes can be captured by finite-state machinery (Karttunen 1993), i.e., computational resources that are accessible to (many) other species. In Fitch's own words: "humans share the processing capabilities required to deal with regular-level sequential processing, and thus phonology, with other animals, and these shared capabilities are implemented in homologous neural processing algorithms and circuitry" (Fitch 2018b).

The flip side of this claim is also something that Fitch has capitalized on: from the statement above it follows that other components of human language that require richer computational resources may constitute examples of evolutionary discontinuity. The prime candidate here is of course natural language syntax, where dependencies require more elaborate memory systems, as Chomsky 1956, 1957 established. Indeed, claims that the sort of computations underlying human language syntax are beyond the reach of other species are frequently made in review articles (e.g., Berwick et al. 2011). It has been called the "syntax barrier", or the "supra-regular boundary" (Fitch 2014, 2018a). Even when it looks like monkeys can break this barrier (Jiang et al. 2018), the discontinuity hypothesis is stated in terms of a much higher *propensity* by humans to build mental hierarchies beyond the reach of finite-state machines (Fitch's Dendrophilia hypothesis; Fitch 2014, 2018a).

Here I would like to argue that in fact one can adopt a perspective where syntax and phonology, and as a result, humans and other animals, exhibit a higher degree of continuity. Sure, they are not identical, but above and beyond the modifications, there is descent, as Darwin would have put it.

My starting point is an observation I made in collaboration with Juan Uriagereka (Boeckx & Uriagereka 2011): when we look at the space available in the "Chomsky hierarchy" of formal languages, and we focus on the portions of it occupied by natural language patterns, it is clear that these patterns are sparsely, as opposed to densely, distributed. The clearest example of this comes from Joshi's observation already mentioned in this chapter that some key grammatical dependencies in language are of the mildly context-sensitive type, they are, as it were, right at the border between context-free and context-sensitive systems. They occupy the lowest rank of the context-sensitive family. Uriagereka and I pointed out that something similar happens at the levels of finite-state and context-free systems: natural language patterns are among the simplest within each class. Why should this be?

I believe that part of the answer can be found in recent work by computational linguist Thomas Graf, whose conclusions I will summarize briefly here (see, e.g., Graf 2014b,a, 2020). Graf's central thesis is that the differences between phonology and syntax are a bit of an illusion. They exist under one perspective, but, importantly for our purposes, dissolve from another perspective. Specifically, the idea that sound patterns are computationally simpler or less demanding (in a quantifiable sense) than sentence patterns (sub-regular vs. supra-regular) relies on the characterization of language patterns as sets of strings. Graf's major point is that if we step away from this characterization and take into account other data structures (e.g., trees, well-known to syntacticians), then the difference between phonology and syntax is far less spectacular. Graf points out that recognizing the set of licit trees (to be exact, Derivation Trees, following the Minimalist Grammar formalism of Stabler 2011) can be accomplished by exploiting the resources of a finite-state automaton. In effect, this simple relativization of data structure (string vs. tree) makes the computational resources for phonology and syntax identical. This is indeed Graf's thesis: no language components require computational resources that fall outside the sub-regular domain. Building on work on phonological patterns by Heinz and collaborators (e.g., Heinz 2018), Graf suggests that this characterization can be further refined: nearly all of these patterns, with principled exceptions, fall into the simple, "strictly local" layer of the "sub-regular" domain.[8] For the sake of completeness I should mention that Graf, following Heinz, argues that some phonological patterns, e.g., harmony processes, are best characterized as being "tierwise strictly local" (requiring representations well-known from autosegmental phonology), and so do syntactic processes such as movement dependencies. Thus, the phonology/syntax parallelism may well be preserved all the way.

For my present purposes, Graf's thesis is very significant: it removes yet another layer of species (or cognitive) discontinuity. If phonology and syntax make use of the same computational resources, and if there is phonological continuity, then there is also syntactic continuity. This of course does not mean that there won't be differences. Phonology is not syntax. Strings and trees are different data structures. But behind these differences, there is a deeply conserved computational architecture that is very simple (and not unique to humans). The differences are variations on a (simple computational, subregular) theme.

Graf's logic achieves two important things for evolutionary studies: First, it illustrates how computational considerations going back to the earliest work in modern linguistics can help identify underlying parallelisms that would be obscured by jargon specific to syntax or phonology in this case. Second, it shows that these distinctions made in the standard formulation of the "Chomsky hierarchy" can be studied in a way that abolishes discontinuity across cognitive

[8]In addition to its relevance for evolutionary considerations, Graf's thesis also has important learnability considerations, bearing directly on some of the problems for the usefulness of the Chomsky hierarchy pointed out in Rogers & Pullum 2011. For relevant discussion, see Lambert et al. 2021.

domains, or species (i.e., it can be studied in a comparative, as opposed to contrastive, mode). As such it can provide operational definitions of linguistic abilities ideally suited for comparative testing in a neurobiological context (see, e.g., Wilson et al. 2017).

When focusing on the phylogeny of syntactic dependencies, it is likely that we will find deeper roots (Petkov & Wilson 2012, Watson et al. 2020, Girard-Buttoz et al. 2021), but also gradual changes pertaining to data structure: hierarchical trees, which I think predated the emergence of *sapiens*, and maybe some autosegmental/tier additions that may be species-specific additions, giving rise to mildly context-sensitive patterns when defined over strings (Malassis et al. 2020). We should welcome such a sharp departure from non-uniformity that all too often still dominates in theoretical linguistics and that was pretty much the "only game in town" not so long ago (Anderson 2004). It's descent with modification all the way down.

4 Richer fossils

For much of their history the language sciences have been dominated by a philological methodology, and a reliance on (narrowly defined) linguistic data. Including in the generative era, when the goal of the enterprise changed dramatically to the cognitive, the methodology remained largely philological, in the sense that traditional linguistic data (words, sentences, etc.) were used to distill cognitive principles, and eventually, one hopes, insights into the nature and content of the biological endowment. Even in more interdisciplinary domains like neurolinguistics or developmental linguistics, traditional data points, in the form of stimuli or child utterances, remain central. But in the absence of such data from the fossil record, or from "non-linguistic" creatures, this methodology comes to a stop.[1]

I find this state of affairs well worth reflecting on, for in a certain sense, it illustrates the limits of a certain research program in linguistics, one that was designed to reach precisely this point of inquiry into the (evolutionary) biological foundations of language. It is perhaps for this reason that Piattelli-Palmarini & Uriagereka 2011 characterized the work on *FOXP2* as "a geneticist's dream", but "a linguist's nightmare". Just when the linguists found themselves confronted with first-rate molecular evidence bearing on our language capacity (Lai et al. 2001), they found their methodology unable to handle it properly. As indicated briefly in chapter 2, since the *FOXP2* discovery over two decades ago, there has been massive progress in many fields whose results bear on language and "the human condition" (i.e., the quintessential focus of generativism, under Chomsky's vision, in my opinion). This provides a unique opportunity for linguists, but it requires a shift in methodology, because in order to exploit all these discoveries (and those yet to come), research in linguistics must proceed in a way that differs sharply from the way it has been done over the last half-century. As they say, in order to dig deeper, one needs a new shovel.

To repeat a key point in chapter 3, I do not mean to throw the baby out with the bathwater. Insights from theoretical linguistics are here to stay. But it is the per-

[1]I am aware of attempts to apply concepts from linguistic theorizing in the analysis of communicative acts in non-human animals (Schlenker et al. 2016, Pleyer & Hartmann 2020). I have not yet been able to see clearly what such approaches could tell us about stages of language evolution whose users went extinct and left no linguistic document to apply these concepts to.

fect time to take seriously Chomsky's assertion that in the future (which I think is now), "it will be necessary to move to a much broader domain of evidence. What linguistics should try to provide is an abstract characterization of (particular and universal) grammar that will serve as a guide and framework for this more general inquiry" (Chomsky 1981). Results concerning the format of rules and representations of the sort I touched on in chapter 3 can indeed guide experimental inquiry seeking to establish linking hypotheses across levels of analysis.

Unlike the early days of generative grammar, the aim is no longer to shift the focus of inquiry (while sticking to standard methodological tools); rather, the aim is to keep the (bio-cognitive) focus, but shift the methodology to give it a more decidedly (recognizable) biological character.

Having more data, from a wide range of sources, certainly helps, but more data does not necessarily provide a fast lane to understanding. To get a good grasp of the biological foundations of language, one must combine "big data" and "big theory". Linguists might feel inadequate when it comes to gathering data "of this new kind", although I think they shouldn't feel that way. Moreover, there is still a vital role for them to play in influencing the design of future experiments, and in interpreting the results of past and current ones.

Sidney Brenner put it best when he wrote: "As was predicted at the beginning of the Human Genome Project, getting the sequence will be the easy part as only technical issues are involved. The hard part will be finding out what it means, because this poses intellectual problems of how to understand the participation of the genes in the functions of living cells" (Brenner 1995). What is true of genes is also true of neural circuits, as Krakauer et al. 2017 rightly stress. Theoretical linguists should not fear engaging with more experimental fields, for as Hopfield pointed out, "too few biologists attempt to deduce broad biological principles from the experimental facts at hand. Indeed the constant quest for new data can distract researchers from the important job of fitting the facts together in a coherent picture."[2]

With these remarks in mind, I would like to provide a brief overview of some of the research opportunities that arise to study language evolution "in the laboratory", as Scott-Phillips & Kirby 2010 put it, or rather "across laboratories", for as we will see, new opportunities require integrating multiple domains of expertise, and no single laboratory can house all of them at once. Certainly, no single individual can be an expert in all of them.

It is likely that the specific illustrations I will use here will quickly become obsolete, so readers should keep their eyes on the main lessons. One key message

[2]https://www.princeton.edu/news/2000/12/15/neuroscience-contest-prompts-thinking-about-thinking

is certainly that it is no longer productive to keep repeating that "the basic difficulty with studying the evolution of language is that the evidence is so sparse" (Jackendoff 2006). Yes, it is true that linguistic behavior does not fossilize, but indirect evidence can exist, especially if we learn about how to manipulate it carefully, avoiding jumping to conclusions, and instead assemble an explanatory chain of argument across levels of analysis. It turns out that aspects of language evolution can be reconstructed. They are not lost forever.

In my own work I have mostly relied on the evidence coming from ancient DNA, which I regard as a game changer. I think that paleogenetics/genomics, together with even more recent work on paleoproteomics, enriches the fossil record significantly. It does not reveal anything immediately about the evolution of cognition, but it provides key elements to reconstruct aspects of brain evolution that in turn can be related to cognitive capacity. This is why work on the neurobiological foundations of language is such a key level of inquiry: it is the main bridge between the molecular data and cognitive science. It is what makes "molecular archaeology" (Pääbo 2014b) possible.

4.1 On language evolution and change

Before embarking on a few illustrations of this line of research, I want to emphasize how the statements above complement (and do not replace or conflict with) work that seeks to find alternative ways to reconstruct language evolution. Here I have in mind the line of work that (in the words of Marieke Schouwstra and Simon Kirby[3]), "grow miniature languages in the lab", by asking people to improvise and communicate with artificial signs. Researchers do so "because [they] want to study how languages can start from scratch, and to see how the languages we know today could have gotten their rules and their rich structure." Such work essentially tries to create the necessary and sufficient conditions for cognitive biases brought to the task by individual learners to modify the raw input of data and shape it in a way that captures key properties of natural languages.

This process of grammar building in the course of interactions (learning/use) is sometimes dismissed as being concerned with processes of language change, not language evolution, since the individuals come to the task already equipped with a human language faculty (Berwick & Chomsky 2016). This criticism can be mitigated by resorting to a complementary method of grammar formation using computational models where the biases of interacting (artificial) agents can be

[3]https://blogs.ed.ac.uk/wegrowlanguages/about

controlled for (Kirby 2001, Thompson et al. 2016). However, critics are quick to point out that this line of work implements the cognitive biases by brute force, and does not show how these evolve organically, as must have happened in the course of (biological) evolution.

I find this type of criticism unfair. To begin with, every experimental method has limitations. *In vitro* work in the life sciences does not attempt to reconstruct all the processes that took place in evolution. The point is to create the conditions that make it possible to isolate at least one factor. Likewise, *in vivo* work with animal models is not claimed to capture all aspects of the species these animals are trying to model. Limitations are opportunities for complementary approaches to arise and fill in the gaps.

As for the claim that what is being studied "in the lab" is language change ("glossogeny") as opposed to language evolution ("phylogeny"), I remain unconvinced, for reasons that I think matter when thinking about language as a biological object of study and how it evolved. On the face of it, the difference can be clearly stated, as Martin Haspelmath has done[4] (see also Mendívil Giró 2019): language evolution refers to the emergence of a cognitive capacity to acquire at least one language, whereas language change refers to the emergence of a new language that differs from the one that preceded it. Crucially, this new language and the one it replaced were both acquired by generations of individuals equipped with the language capacity whose evolution is the central topic of "language evolution". Put differently, one domain of research studies the difference between a non-linguistic creature and a linguistic creature, whereas the other domain of research focuses on how different generations of linguistic creatures exercise their (by hypothesis, invariant) language capacity. But to my mind researchers framing the issue in this way have underestimated the difficulty of a new question that arises by doing so: What is a linguistic creature once we recognize (as discussed earlier in this essay) that language is an evolutionary mosaic?

It seems to me that many of the researchers who insist upon a sharp separation between language evolution and language change also insist (tacitly) on a sharp contrast between "us" (humans) and the other animals (some kind of "FLN"). That is to say, the distinction between language phylogeny and glossogeny is not theory-free and goes well beyond somewhat arbitrary decisions about lexical conventions (evolution vs. change).

In a world where the notion of language is fixed[5] (as in the orthodox characterization of "Universal Grammar"), the distinction between language evolution and

[4]https://dlc.hypotheses.org/894

[5]One where humans are still seen as the pinnacle of evolution?

language change appears to be a no-brainer. But if the concept of language is far less uniform, biologically speaking–in other words, if the concept of language leaks (across species)–, then the gap between linguistic and non-linguistic creatures is reduced (dramatically so in the case of our closest relatives with whom we interbred), and once this gap is reduced, so is the gap between (the processes underlying) language evolution and language change. What emerges instead is a much more gradual picture or continuum for language, pretty much like the one already entertained for key aspects of language such as vocal learning (Petkov & Jarvis 2012, Martins & Boeckx 2020b).

Instead of thinking of the language faculty as a trait that emerged abruptly, and that did not change once it emerged (Berwick & Chomsky 2016), I find it more useful to think of our language capacity as a collection of (generic) cognitive biases (Christiansen & Chater 2016, Gervain & Mehler 2010)[6] put to the task of acquiring and using "an art", as Darwin 1871 defined our "language instinct". Such biases may be more or less "primitive" (widely shared across species) or "derived" (substantially modified over the course of evolution of our lineage),[7] but without a sharp discontinuity from the cognitive capacities of our ancestors and living relatives (contra Hauser et al. 2002, as we saw in chapter 3). As such, the picture that emerges is not radically different from the cognitive continuity observed across the communities of language users that constitute the focus on research on language change. The changes may look more or less dramatic but that is more a subjective (non-theory-free) assessment than an objective truth.

While it is tempting to define our "modern" human language capacity as the full collection of cognitive biases that reliably leads to the acquisition and use of natural languages, I doubt that this statement is either necessary or sufficient. It is not necessary because perhaps not all biases are absolutely needed to reliably learn a language, and it is not sufficient, because talk of cognitive biases too quickly leads one to think of "internal" factors, at the expense of "external" factors.

The constructive role of the environment (the context of acquisition and use[8]) may well contribute significantly to the reliable emergence of properties once

[6] I do not think we yet have a very good idea of what this catalog of cognitive biases may consist of. I suspect there are likely to be very many, associated with general notions like memory, attention, salience, etc.

[7] In other words, the emergence of some biases may depend on particular anatomical developments (brain growth trajectory, etc.).

[8] Acquisition and use are not different things. Acquisition is use with a greater degree of uncertainty (McCauley & Christiansen 2019), much as evolution is akin to building an airplane while flying it.

too quickly built into "Universal Grammar" (and attributed "ultimately" to the genome) (Kirby 2017, Raviv 2020), so much so that the environment may act as a buffer and compensate for a large amount of biological variation among language learners. In other words, it may be that some cognitive biases are not so necessary,[9] with effects felt only in "exceptional" circumstances of acquisition and use. After all, even "core" aspects of language may come from *tendencies* (e.g. the "dendrophilia" hypothesis in Fitch 2014 mentioned in chapter 3 and defined as a propensity for hierarchical structuring), rather than hard, all-or-nothing constraints. There may be a fair amount of redundancy among biases.

Over and above computational models and more realistic experimental settings, the literature on emerging sign languages makes clear that the "arena of use" (to use a phrase from Hurford's lucid and prescient essay; Hurford 1990) matters in shaping grammars,[10] and reveals that one should not insist (contra Mendívil Giró 2019) on a radical separation between language evolution and language change, not because[11] "language emergence" ("The change from a very simple system into a system that is 'characteristically linguistic'") is a third, middle-ground scenario, but because the notion of "characteristically linguistic" is much harder to define in a Darwinian context than it is in a "Cartesian" context (Chomsky 1966).

Consider for instance the grammatical differences between the songs of white-rumped munias and the songs of Bengalese finches. As is well-known thanks to the groundbreaking work of Kazuo Okanoya (Okanoya 2004, 2017), the domesticated strain of the munia, known as the Bengalese finch, exhibits greater song variation and complexity (greater variation in transition between notes, making the structure of the munia song more linear). If we were to refer to these song repertoires as "languages", would we treat the change in song structure from the munia to the finch as a case of language evolution or language change? That there are genetic differences between the wild munia and the domesticated Bengalese finch would maybe lead one to talk about language evolution, although the core song circuit of the Bengalese finch does not differ in fundamental ways from that of the munia. The environmental context clearly differs, and so perhaps one would speak of new song emergence, or song change. In the case of differences like Middle English vs Modern English, few doubt that we are dealing with a case of language change, but I think that our faltering intuitions about

[9]They could be said to be defeasible (in a sense reminding one abstractly of how grammar is organized according to Optimality Theory, Smolensky & Prince 2004).

[10]Consider also works showing how different environmental conditions correlate with certain typological properties, e.g. Everett et al. 2015.

[11]Contra T. Scott-Phillips, in https://dlc.hypotheses.org/894.

evolution or change in the munia vs. Bengalese finch situation point to these processes occupying a continuum. This very much matters for the treatment of language *evolution*, in light of the growing evidence that a fair amount of "language-readiness" must have been in place in the common ancestor we shared with the Neanderthals (Dediu & Levinson 2013).

Consider another scenario. It has been claimed that aspects of our biology (jaw size, vocal tract configuration, possible brain-related mutations harbored by microcephaly candidate genes like *ASPM*; Dediu et al. 2017, Blasi et al. 2019, Dediu & Ladd 2007, Dediu 2021) may impact typological properties of our language (e.g., presence of certain classes of consonants, or tonal contrasts). Given the relevance of biological mutations, would we speak of language evolution? Is the difference between a system with certain consonants or with tone "enough" to qualify as language evolution, or do we take these differences to still fall within a certain type of linguistic system and speak of language change instead? Would our intuition carry over to situations of, say, pervasive congenital deafness in a population forcing a modality change in the way the language users communicate? Perhaps we would still say that the "underlying" system remains the same, but aren't transitions from a gesture-dominant to a speech-dominant system treated as language evolution in the "protolanguage" literature (Fitch 2010)? This is particularly important in light of the Darwinian take on selection, which necessarily works on standing variation.

There are of course non-cognitive (philological) ways of studying language change that look totally inadequate when applied to language evolution, but it seems to me that if one adopts a cognitive approach to language change, one that focuses on process rather than state (Heine & Kuteva 2002), then the most sensible approach is to drop any sharp dividing line between change and evolution, and view "linguistic" differences across species and communities along a continuum.

I have sometimes heard[12] that choosing to focus on the "biological" foundations or the "cultural" foundations of language is a bit like the two ways of viewing the Necker cube: both are valid perspectives. But I think this is the wrong metaphor to use, as it suggests that you must do one or the other (our visual system does not let you entertain both perspectives at the same time). Instead, if, as I suggest here, one must bear in mind the neurobiological foundations of cultural learning as well as the role of culture in giving meaning and direction to the learning biases we are endowed with, then the biological/cultural divide is more like another optical illusion: the Penrose triangle, i.e., an impossibility.

[12] I recall the Necker cube metaphor being used in this sense by T. Scott-Phillips in one of his presentations.

Part of the resistance towards the view advocated here may stem from the failure on the part of the generative tradition to recognize the critical, structuring socio-cultural aspect of core properties of language (this is especially true in the domain of syntax). One may insist on language being "for thought" and not "for communication", as Chomsky and followers have done, but clearly language exists, and survives, thanks to its communal use. There is no faculty of language that is not instantiated in and by a specific language used by more than one language user. There is no "parameter" that can be set without cues from usage data. It is just wrong to say that language evolution is about the evolution of a mental organ, whereas language change is about the way in which this organ is put to use. They are not dissociable things: an organ without use is no organ at all. True, external stimuli don't contain "grammar", but nor does the genome.

4.2 Self-domestication

Part of the reason why I have devoted a fair amount of research time to the topic of "self-domestication" is precisely because it offers a very concrete way to understand better the interaction between biological and cultural evolution. Self-domestication refers to the hypothesis that humans (specifically, *Homo sapiens*) went through a process similar to that which morphed wolves into dogs, and that this matters for understanding human cognition and indeed some aspects of our language faculty. This process is, I think, best characterized as a reduction in reactive aggression (Wrangham 2018). To strengthen the case for self-domestication, it is usually pointed out (Theofanopoulou, Gastaldon, et al. 2017) that anatomical changes in our lineage are reminiscent of a set of phenotypical traits that tend to characterize domesticated species, collectively referred to as the "domestication syndrome" (Wilkins et al. 2014): reductions in skull and brain size, changes to braincase shape, reductions in tooth size, shortening of the muzzle/flattening of the face, and the development of floppy ears.

Self-domestication is hypothesized to have contributed to our ultra-social phenotype (Hare 2017). Crucially, for present purposes, this change in temperament modified the context in which humans communicated, learned from one another, and shared knowledge.

As Thomas 2014 put it, as soon as we recognize the importance of cultural transmission for language evolution, it becomes important to ask about the origin of the traits that enabled that "process of structure-creating cultural evolution" (Thomas & Kirby 2018). Eventually, this question leads to the neurobiological foundations of specific cognitive (learning) biases. Thus, cultural evolution and biological evolution cannot be kept distinct for long; there are clear feedback loops between the two. Self-domestication is a hypothesis regarding these neurobiological foundations.

Work on self-domestication over the past five years or so illustrates a handful of themes that reveal how much has changed in the context of language evolution.

Until recently, the most successful branch of evolutionary linguistics from a comparative perspective was clearly the literature on vocal learning. Though rare among animals, vocal (production) learning (ability to modify vocal output based on experience) is not an ability unique to humans, and its existence in at least a few species has led to some impressive results at multiple levels of analysis, not only at the behavioral level, or developmental level, but also right down to neurogenetics (for a survey, see Jarvis 2019). I believe the self-domestication hypothesis opens the door to similar progress, now that there is a growing database of paleogenomes allowing one to probe the earliest stages of domestication, as well as a growing understanding of the neurological bases of tameness, which is the central unifying trait of domesticates.

To be sure, progress does not entail lack of controversy: even in the domain of vocal learning, which builds on decades on intensive investigation, the exact set of vocal learners is still up for grabs, and the necessary and sufficient neurological mechanisms are still a matter of debate (Martins & Boeckx 2020b). The same is to be expected for the self-domestication hypothesis. Work over the past 5 years has been driven by an influential hypothesis (the neural crest based hypothesis put forth by Wilkins et al. 2014) that ties the domestication syndrome (traits associated with tameness) to a mild neural crest deficit ('neurocristopathy'), conceptually similar to the role played by the hypothesis that vocal production learning depends on a direct cortico-laryngeal connection (Jürgens-Kuypers hypothesis, as per Fitch 2010. Both hypotheses are contested (Lord et al. 2020, Johnsson et al. 2021, Lameira 2017), but what is not up for debate is their usefulness in shaping experimental work (Pfenning et al. 2014, Zanella et al. 2019, Wilkins et al. 2021).

There may well be multiple paths to vocal learning (multiple mechanisms at work) (Martins & Boeckx 2020b, Wirthlin et al. 2019), just as different stages of domestication may require distinct explanations (O'Rourke & Boeckx 2020). It is likely that for both vocal learning and domestication the notion of "continuum" will be needed. This is just the fractal nature of scientific explanation at work. What matters, and what is the true sign of progress, is that it is now possible to move beyond claims that language is exclusive to us, and that careful experimental testing can be carried out.

Working on the self-domestication hypothesis has taught me several important lessons. First, it is possible to join forces, working across laboratories, to validate *in vitro* hypotheses first generated *in silico*. In my particular case, a close look at genetic differences between domesticates and their closest wild relatives (Theofanopoulou, Gastaldon, et al. 2017) and between modern humans and their closest extinct relations (Kuhlwilm & Boeckx 2019) led us to zoom in on a region of the genome implicated in various neurodevelopmental disorders including the Williams-Beuren syndrome (known to give rise to a hypersocial phenotype), and study the impact of differential expression of a gene called *BAZ1B* in neural crest development (Zanella et al. 2019). Though it is by no means the only relevant gene, we argued that it contributed to the retraction of the modern human face, which may thus underlie key traits of the domestication syndrome.

In subsequent work (Andirkó et al. 2021) we tested the claim that the modern human face emerges significantly earlier than other aspects of our "modern" anatomy, such as our characteristically globular braincase (Hublin et al. 2017). The central message of this work is that the *sapiens* lineage has a more complex evolutionary history than previously assumed (see also Scerri et al. 2018, Bergström et al. 2021), and that quite a few important things happened in the nearly 500k years after the split from the Neanderthals and the Denisovans (Stringer 2016). Accordingly, if at least some of the changes impacted cognition and our language capacity, as I currently think they did, they add dimensions of variation in the context of the "antiquity" of the language faculty (Dediu & Levinson 2013): there is a lot of hypothesis space between "exclusively" modern/recent evolutionary changes and "shared with our closest extinct relatives". All of this contributes to a significantly more gradual narrative for language evolution.

Our attempt to pinpoint genetic changes associated with self-domestication (Theofanopoulou, Gastaldon, et al. 2017), has also taught me that although the initial focus may be on the domestication syndrome, presumably the result of mutations impacting the neural crest, other changes, at the level of the brain, particularly those harbored by various receptors regulating stress circuits (glutamate receptors, oxytocin receptors) likely played a crucial role (O'Rourke & Boeckx 2020, Theofanopoulou, Boeckx & Jarvis 2017) in giving rise to the cognitive biases that became part of our "domesticated phenotype" (reduction in reactive aggression being in my opinion the most important one). Accordingly, when trying to model *in vitro* some of the aspects of self-domestication, both the "face" and the "brain" and how these two interface must be taken into account. Our best bet right now (ongoing work with with Alessandro Vitriolo and Giuseppe Testa) is neuruloids, the organoid structures designed by Haremaki et al. 2019 to capture the developmental stages at which brain and face are about to embark on distinct trajectories. At bottom, we are trying to understand how *sapiens* grew a small face, but maintained a big brain.

It is true that some of this experimental work may seem remote from linguistic concerns. But one must bear in mind the indirect connection between genotype and phenotype. The paleogenetic revolution opens the door to an unprecedented range of experimental opportunities to shed light on the human condition (Pääbo 2014b), but it in no way reduces the gap between genes and cognition. As a result, we must learn to carefully and patiently build linking hypotheses step by step, and understand that for many of these steps, the overall shape of the explanatory link won't be obvious. The same is true in architecture: it took a long time for the outline of the Eiffel tower to emerge from the scaffoldings. It would have been a mistake to try to speed things up just to make the end result more transparent more quickly.

Still, in the context of self-domestication, we are beginning to understand how changes at the level of neurotransmitters impact specific circuits (especially the basal ganglia) that help us understand how the songs of the (domesticated) Bengalese finches become more varied, and in some sense more complex than the songs of the wild munias (O'Rourke et al. 2021). It is also clear that changes of facial morphology, e.g., the disappearance of prominent browridges, opened up new possibilities for facial expressions, reshaping social dynamics (Godinho et al. 2018) and communication that must be understood in a multi-modal context. If social pressures truly impact grammatical structure (as evidenced in Raviv 2020), then the changes in social dynamics brought about by self-domestication must have modified our language capacity (in ways that could be revealed by work on other domesticates not known for vocal learning, such as dogs, bonobos, etc.).

4.3 Brain development

As stated above, there is evidence that our facial phenotype evolved earlier than other aspects of our cranium. In particular, our species-specific globular skull shape emerged in the last 100k years (Neubauer et al. 2018). I have long been interested in this characteristic skull shape (Boeckx 2013, Boeckx & Benítez-Burraco 2014), because much like facial reduction and retraction, which are potentially linked to a change in social cognition ('the self-domestication hypothesis'), a globular neurocranium points to a distinct perinatal brain growth trajectory in our species (Gunz et al. 2010). Whereas the face of a *sapiens* newborn is already characteristically "small", and "modern-looking", it takes longer for the neurocranium to acquire its distinctive shape, and regional brain growth changes appear to be the primary determinant.

Phillip Gunz, Jean-Jacques Hublin and colleagues have suggested that late-expanding, posterior structures like the cerebellum played a major role in this reshaping (Hublin et al. 2015).[13] Together with a few other structures, namely the precuneus/superior parietal area (Pereira-Pedro et al. 2020, Bruner 2021), the cerebellum stands out in the context of *sapiens* brain evolution (see also Dumas et al. 2021, Weiss et al. 2021, Gunz et al. 2019).

The derived status of the cerebellum raises a lot of interesting new questions in the context of language evolution. To begin with, the modern-specific cerebellar expansion appears to be more pronounced for the right hemisphere (Kochiyama et al. 2018), and given that this is the dominant cerebellar hemisphere for language functions, it raises the possibility that this anatomical trait had cognitive import of great relevance for us. The fact that we can already identify candidate mutations for this differential growth of the cerebellum provides yet another piece of evidence for the truly transformative role of paleogenetics: even without ancient genomes, one could single out the cerebellum (as Gunz et al. 2010 did on the basis of detailed virtual reconstructions of endocasts), but genetic information opens the possibility of going beyond size criteria and attributing differential growth trajectories to specific cellular phenotypes.

In the context of the cerebellum, the granule cells constitute our best bet so far for a candidate cell population that may explain this cerebellar enlargement. This is important because such information can guide further inquiry: the question changes from "What can an enlarged cerebellum do?" to something more precise about the role of an expanded granular layer. For instance, Straub et al. 2020 point to an increased storage capacity associated with an expanded granular layer in mammals, opening up the possibility of amplified representational capacities in our species. Could this have led to an expanded range of representations (cf. our discussion of Graf's hypothesis in chapter 3), modulating cortical output in our species, adding tiers to the strictly local tree-based representations constructed in the temporo-frontal network linked by an expanded direct arcuate tract (Rilling et al. 2008, Friederici 2017, Eichert et al. 2019, Balezeau et al.

[13]In our work, building on (paleo)genetic datasets, we indeed find evidence for this claim: "modern"-derived, nearly fixed expression quantitative trait loci accumulate in the cerebellum more than in other structures, in a way that is statistically significant (Andirkó & Boeckx 2019). Regions of the modern genome associated with signals of positive selection and embedded in larger introgression deserts (regions depleted of introgressed variants from other hominins) have a distinctive expression profile in the cerebellum (Buisan et al. 2021), and finally machine-learning approaches assigning an age of emergence to nearly-fixed mutations in the modern genome point to an enrichment for the cerebellum around 90kya (Andirkó et al. 2021).

2020)? Such questions highlight the need to investigate an "extended" language network, well beyond the classical (Broca's and Wernicke's) regions.

The evidence pointing to a distinctive role of the cerebellum also raises important new questions for comparative neuroscience, where the cerebellum is still all too frequently left out of the equation, as is the case for our circuit-level characterization of vocal learning, with only a few exceptions (Pidoux et al. 2018, Hoeksema et al. 2021, Wirthlin et al. 2018, Gutiérrez-Ibáñez et al. 2018). The same is true for developmental neuroscience, where certain (posterior) brain regions may be more important than previously thought (witness Orpella et al. 2020, Irurtzun 2015).

Last, but not least, it forces one to think about what the behavioral-cognitive contribution of these neuroanatomical changes was: now that we have a better appreciation of capacities of other hominins, are there some behavioral practices that could be imputed to these changes? I suspect that there are. If the brain grows differently, it wires differently, and thus functions distinctively. Providing detailed linking hypotheses addressing these questions is an important task for the years to come.

One of the interesting possibilities emerging from the different timing of modified ontogenies for the face and the brain is that the two-stage hypothesis put forward in (Okanoya 2017) to capture the structural differences between the songs of the Bengalese finches and those of the munias (first, a domestication/taming phase, followed by a sexual selection phase resulting in more varied and elaborate songs for the Bengalese finches) may guide hypothesis-construction for human language evolution. Could the self-domestication phase set the stage for further elaboration, made possible by changes in specific brain structures? How could this be tested?

4.4 Language-ready "mini-brains"?

To my mind one of the most exciting possibilities for evolutionary studies arises in the context of impressive progress in the field of synthetic embryology, or, as it is more popularly known, of "organoids". Organoids are three-dimensional culture systems consisting initially of homogeneous populations of stem cells that "self-organize" in complex ways. As they do so, they produce patterns that are similar to those found *in vivo* during embryogenesis. As such, they offer manipulable "miniaturized" model systems of organs (Huch et al. 2017).

Thanks to the rapid advances in "brain organoid" studies (beginning with Lancaster et al. 2013), it is now possible to consider that aspects of our language-ready brain, especially those that arise early in development, may be examined and manipulated in an experimental context. This is particularly the case when combined with the use of gene-editing techniques ('CRISPR-cas9') to model in three dimensions the effects of variants found in species whose brains are otherwise lost to us forever, as is the case for the Neanderthals and Denisovans (Trujillo et al. 2021). In a way, such work would complement the efforts by evolutionary linguists to grow mini-languages in the lab.

Comparative work on brain organoids using closely related species such as chimpanzees and bonobos has already made interesting discoveries (Mora-Bermúdez et al. 2016, Kanton et al. 2019), but up to now it has mostly focused on cortical aspects, and sought to model factors that led to cortical expansion in the *Homo* lineage (Heide et al. 2018, Pollen et al. 2019). As discussed above, for *sapiens*-specific aspects, we will need to develop new organoid models (most molecular events associated with cortical expansion are present in all hominin genomes currently available; Florio et al. 2018). But it strikes me that there is a genuine possibility to capture aspects of human brain development *in vitro* (Giandomenico & Lancaster 2017, Muchnik et al. 2019, Benito-Kwiecinski et al. 2021). For instance, it is now possible to generate "assembloids" (fused organoids made up of distinct parts) for cortico-striatum structures (Miura et al. 2020) and cortico-spinal cord-muscle structures (Andersen et al. 2020). Both structures figure prominently in discussion of vocal learning (Jarvis 2019), and I think it is not unreasonable to anticipate that the assembloids just mentioned will enable us to probe the development of circuitry that provides the neurobiological foundations for speech.

To be sure, organoid technology is not without challenges (reproducibility being the major one) or limitations (it can only capture the very early developmental stages, and it can as of now only test the effect of a few mutations at a time), but this is true of all models, and we should take advantage of the opportunities they offer. In particular, the (still distant) hope of constructing "giant" assembloids bringing together some of the most derived aspects of human brain development could provide a decisive step in "brain-gene-ering"[14] the evolution of the language-ready brain.

To be very clear, the point is not to expect these organoids to "speak", but rather to reconstruct key aspects of the neurobiological scaffolding of our linguistic ability that the fossil record is inherently incapable of capturing. By exploiting paleogenetic information to grow brain organoids with ancestral mutations in them, we can, as it were, enrich the fossil record, and avoid the facile conclusion

[14]https://braingeneers.ucsc.edu

that "languages don't fossilize". Aspects of brain development making language possible may be reconstructed from an expanded fossil record.

In so doing, we would be contributing to the "exciting challenge" laid out in Fisher 2014: "to distil all these As, Gs, Ts, and Cs into meaningful insights regarding the biological underpinnings of some of our most mysterious traits, such as speech and language. By taking advantage of an ever-growing tool kit for investigating gene function, it will at last be possible to bridge the mechanistic gaps between DNA, neurons, circuits, brains, and cognition."

5 Another "bio-linguistics" is possible

One need not be an expert in word formation to figure out that prefixes alter meaning. A post-doctoral position is not the same thing as a doctoral position; a preview is not the same thing as a view; to outplay is not the same thing as to play. The addition of a prefix matters. Accordingly, one should expect some added meaning value when we see the prefix "bio-" applied to terms proper to the language sciences, including the very notion of "bio-linguistics". Yet, I do not think that the theoretical linguistics literature that professes a biological orientation and waves the banner of "biolinguistics" offers a fair reflection of the difficulty one quickly encounters when one tries to do genuine interdisciplinary work combining "bio" and linguistics. If the biological commitment of the field were really taken seriously, many linguistics papers would look quite different. There would be a lot more constructive discussion about the brain, there would be a lot more serious talk about other species, and there would also be a lot less about physical laws in language design, as well as far fewer hand-waving remarks about the "genetic endowment".

While no one can seriously doubt that there is something about our biology that makes it possible for us to develop and use grammatical systems we call natural languages, there is no denying that the generative tradition explored a specific way of characterizing this "biological endowment": a rich set of domain-specific cognitive properties that together form what is widely known as "Universal Grammar" (UG). This is where the controversy really arises. Lots of scientists object to this characterization of the biological endowment. They favor domain-general solutions, and differ in the degree to which they see learning and environmental interactions shaping the mature linguistic knowledge in humans. In my view, to the extent one is interested in characterizing this biological endowment, one is doing biolinguistics. One need not be an orthodox UG advocate to be a biolinguist. I mean this in two ways: first, one can be a biolinguist even if one rejects the existence of domain-specific cognitive primitives in the language domain. Second, the mere fact of appealing to UG to account for certain facts about our linguistic knowledge does not make one a biolinguist.

There has never been a better time to focus on this biological endowment, given the amount of relevant data currently waiting to be confronted, tested, and interpreted. Linguists ought to play a much more active role in this enterprise, if only to preserve the import of the insights of the cognitive revolution of the 1950s.

To my mind, Eric Lenneberg, who did so much to get the field of "biolinguistics" off the ground, put it best, when he wrote: "Nothing is gained by labeling the propensity for language as biological unless we can use this insight for new research directions – unless more specific correlates can be uncovered" (Lenneberg 1967).

In the preface of *Biological foundations of language*, Lenneberg expressed his feeling that biology had been "badly neglected" in language studies. I think this is still true today, even among those who appeal to biology in the introductory remarks to their works. In the same preface Lenneberg refers to Meader and Muyskens's *Handbook of biolinguistics* (Meader & Muyskens 1950) but points out that he was aiming at a "distinct theoretical position" from the one found in that work. As a result, he did not endorse the term "biolinguistics" there, to avoid confusion. Perhaps he still would resist the term now, as I have come to do, in light of the way it is used by linguists who make so little contact with data generated by biologists (for further discussion and relevant quotes, see Martins & Boeckx 2016). I suspect Lenneberg would prefer a term like "cognitive biology of language" to describe a discipline where the formal nature of language is recognized (as it was in the appendix to Lenneberg 1967, authored by Chomsky), as it must be if reductive biases are to be avoided, but necessarily translated in ways that admit empirical tests of the sort (other) biologists perform. For, like every interdisciplinary enterprise, "biolinguistics" is both a goldmine (lots of new opportunities and "low-hanging fruit") and a minefield (ideas lost in translation).

Doing biolinguistics means inhabiting an "interfield". It means being willing to sit between a rock (biologists' naïve notions of language) and a hard place (linguists' naïve notions of biology). It means building bridges. Bridges for ideas to travel on. As everyone knows, bridge-builders have to work as part of a team; they cannot do it on their own. In addition to figuring out which material to use for the bridge, they have to become deeply acquainted with the nature of the soil of both sides to be united; they have to have an understanding of the landscape, and the flow of traffic around the areas that will be united by the bridge. In this sense, bridge-builders are a bit like translators, who have to know more than one language, but also have to familiarize themselves with the cultures these languages are spoken in. Biolinguists are like that, too. They have to link, and therefore know two fields. They may not need to know everything about both fields. But they must know enough to convey messages back and forth, and make ideas flow in both directions.

Like translators, "biolinguists" may always be recognizable by their accents when they move in a culture that is not originally theirs, but the translation exercise is something fundamental, no matter how imperfect it may appear to the natives. Here is what Tim Parks has to say about the added value of translation in his essay "Gained in Translation"):[1]

> Translators are people who read books for us. Tolstoy wrote in Russian, so someone must read him for us and then write down that reading in our language. Since the book will be fuller and richer the more experience a reader brings to it, we would want our translator, as he or she reads, to be aware of as much as possible, aware of cultural references, aware of lexical patterns, aware of geographical setting and historical moment. Aware, too, of our own language and its many resources. Far from being "just subjective", these differences will be a function of the different experiences these readers bring to the book, since none of us accumulates the same experience. Even then, of course, two expert translators will very likely produce two quite different versions. But if what we want is a translation of Tolstoy, rather than just something that sounds good enough sentence by sentence, it would seem preferable to have our reading done for us by people who can bring more, rather than less, to the work.

Lenneberg gave us the seeds of an alternative, richer, bio-linguistic program. Today, such seeds find much more fertile ground than they did fifty years ago. Linguists would be wrong to let others reap the fruits just by keeping their methodological blinders on. If we believe that the target of linguistic theorizing is "ultimately biology", there is no alternative to going there, and doing some actual biology. What was a logical problem ("Darwin's [Problem]") must find a biological (Darwinian) solution.

[1]https://www.nybooks.com/daily/2017/12/09/gained-in-translation

References

Andersen, Jimena, Omer Revah, Yuki Miura, Nicholas Thom, Neal D. Amin, Kevin W. Kelley, Mandeep Singh, Xiaoyu Chen, Mayuri Vijay Thete, Elisabeth M. Walczak, et al. 2020. Generation of functional human 3D cortico-motor assembloids. *Cell* 183(7). 1913–1929.e26.

Anderson, Stephen R. 2004. *Doctor Dolittle's delusion*. New Haven, CT: Yale University Press.

Andirkó, Alejandro & Cedric Boeckx. 2019. Derived Homo sapiens cis-eQTL regulation: Implications for brain evolution. *bioRxiv*. 771816.

Andirkó, Alejandro, Juan Moriano, Alessandro Vitriolo, Martin Kuhlwilm, Giuseppe Testa & Cedric Boeckx. 2021. Fine-grained temporal mapping of derived high-frequency variants supports the mosaic nature of the evolution of Homo sapiens. *bioRxiv*. 2021.01.22.427608.

Balezeau, Fabien, Benjamin Wilson, Guillermo Gallardo, Fred Dick, William Hopkins, Alfred Anwander, Angela D. Friederici, Timothy D. Griffiths & Christopher I. Petkov. 2020. Primate auditory prototype in the evolution of the arcuate fasciculus. *Nature neuroscience* 23(5). 611–614.

Benito-Kwiecinski, Silvia, Stefano L. Giandomenico, Magdalena Sutcliffe, Erlend S. Riis, Paula Freire-Pritchett, Iva Kelava, Stephanie Wunderlich, Ulrich Martin, Gregory A.Wray, KateMcDole & Madeline A.Lancaster. 2021. An early cell shape transition drives evolutionary expansion of the human forebrain. *Cell* 184(8). 2084–2102.e19.

Bergström, A., C. Stringer, M. Hajdinjak, E. Scerri & P. Skoglund. 2021. Origins of modern human ancestry. *Nature* 590. 229–237.

Berwick, Robert C. & Noam Chomsky. 2016. *Why only us: Language and evolution*. Cambridge, Mass.: MIT press.

Berwick, Robert C. & Noam Chomsky. 2019. All or nothing: No half-Merge and the evolution of syntax. *PLoS biology* 17(11). e3000539.

Berwick, Robert C., Kazuo Okanoya, Gabriel JL Beckers & Johan J. Bolhuis. 2011. Songs to syntax: The linguistics of birdsong. *Trends in cognitive sciences* 15(3). 113–121.

Bickerton, Derek. 1984. The language bioprogram hypothesis. *Behavioral and brain sciences* 7(2). 173–188.

Blasi, Damián E., Steven Moran, Scott R. Moisik, Paul Widmer, Dan Dediu & Balthasar Bickel. 2019. Human sound systems are shaped by post-Neolithic changes in bite configuration. *Science* 363(6432). eaav3218.

Bloomfield, Tiffany C., Timothy Q. Gentner & Daniel Margoliash. 2011. What birds have to say about language. *Nature neuroscience* 14(8). 947.

Boeckx, Cedric. 2006. *Linguistic minimalism: Origins, concepts, methods, and aims.* Oxford: Oxford University Press.

Boeckx, Cedric. 2009. *Language in cognition: Uncovering mental structures and the rules behind them.* Hoboken: John Wiley & Sons.

Boeckx, Cedric. 2013. Biolinguistics: Forays into human cognitive biology. *Journal of Anthropological Sciences* 91. 1–28.

Boeckx, Cedric. 2016. Review of Ljiljana Progovac, Evolutionary syntax (Oxford studies in the evolution of language). Oxford: Oxford university press, 2015. Pp. Xv+ 261. *Journal of Linguistics* 52(2). 476–480.

Boeckx, Cedric. 2017. Not only us. *Inference Intern. Rev. Sci* 3. 1.

Boeckx, Cedric & Antonio Benítez-Burraco. 2014. The shape of the human language-ready brain. *Frontiers in psychology* 5. 282.

Boeckx, Cedric & Juan Uriagereka. 2011. Biolinguistics and information. In George Terzis & Robert Arp (eds.), *Information and living systems: Philosophical and scientific perspectives*, 353–370. Cambridge, Mass.: MIT Press.

Brenner, Sydney. 1995. Loose end. *Current Biology* 5(1). 94.

Bromberger, Sylvain & Morris Halle. 1989. Why phonology is different. *Linguistic inquiry* 20(1). 51–70.

Bruner, Emiliano. 2021. Evolving human brains: Paleoneurology and the fate of Middle Pleistocene. *Journal of Archaeological Method and Theory* 28. 76–94.

Buisan, Raül, Juan Moriano, Alejandro Andirkó & Cedric Boeckx. 2021. A distinct expression profile in the cerebellum and striatum for genes under selection within introgression deserts. *bioRxiv*. 2021.03.26.437167.

Chomsky, Noam. 1956. Three models for the description of language. *IRE Transactions on information theory* 2(3). 113–124.

Chomsky, Noam. 1957. *Syntactic structures.* The Hague: Mouton.

Chomsky, Noam. 1959. A review of BF skinner's verbal behavior. *Language* 35(1). 26–58.

Chomsky, Noam. 1966. *Cartesian linguistics: A chapter in the history of rationalist thought.* Cambridge: Cambridge University Press.

Chomsky, Noam. 1978. *Rules and representations.* New York: Columbia University Press.

Chomsky, Noam. 1981. *Lectures on government and binding: The pisa lectures.* Berlin: Walter de Gruyter.

Chomsky, Noam. 1986. *Knowledge of language: Its nature, origin, and use.* New York: Praeger.

Chomsky, Noam. 2000. *New horizons in the study of language and mind.* Cambridge: Cambridge University Press.

Chomsky, Noam. 2004. Beyond explanatory adequacy. In Adriana Belletti (ed.), *The cartography of syntactic structures: Structures and beyond*, 104–131. Oxford: Oxford University Press.

Chomsky, Noam. 2012. *The science of language: Interviews with James McGilvray.* Cambridge: Cambridge University Press.

Christiansen, Morten H. & Nick Chater. 2016. *Creating language: Integrating evolution, acquisition, and processing.* Cambridge, Mass.: MIT Press.

Cisek, Paul. 2019. Resynthesizing behavior through phylogenetic refinement. *Attention, Perception, & Psychophysics* 81(7). 2265–2287.

Cornish, Hannah, Kenny Smith & Simon Kirby. 2013. Systems from sequences: An iterated learning account of the emergence of systematic structure in a non-linguistic task. In *Proceedings of the Annual Meeting of the Cognitive Science Society*, vol. 35.

Darwin, Charles. 1871. *The descent of man and selection in relation to sex.* Vol. 1. London: D. Appleton.

de Boer, Bart, Bill Thompson, Andrea Ravignani & Cedric Boeckx. 2020. Evolutionary dynamics do not motivate a single-mutant theory of human language. *Scientific reports* 10(1). 1–9.

Dediu, Dan. 2021. Tone and genes: New cross-linguistic data and methods support the weak negative effect of the "derived" allele of ASPM on tone, but not of Microcephalin. *Plos one* 16(6). e0253546.

Dediu, Dan, Rick Janssen & Scott R. Moisik. 2017. Language is not isolated from its wider environment: Vocal tract influences on the evolution of speech and language. *Language & Communication* 54. 9–20.

Dediu, Dan & D. Robert Ladd. 2007. Linguistic tone is related to the population frequency of the adaptive haplogroups of two brain size genes, ASPM and Microcephalin. *Proceedings of the National Academy of Sciences* 104(26). 10944–10949.

Dediu, Dan & Stephen C. Levinson. 2013. On the antiquity of language: The reinterpretation of Neandertal linguistic capacities and its consequences. *Frontiers in psychology* 4. 397.

Dediu, Dan & Stephen C. Levinson. 2018. Neanderthal language revisited: Not only us. *Current Opinion in Behavioral Sciences* 21. 49–55.

Den Hoed, Joery, Karthikeyan Devaraju & Simon E. Fisher. 2021. Molecular networks of the FOXP2 transcription factor in the brain. *EMBO Reports* 22(8). e52803.

de Waal, Frans BM & Pier Francesco Ferrari. 2010. Towards a bottom-up perspective on animal and human cognition. *Trends in cognitive sciences* 14(5). 201–207.

Dobzhansky, Theodosius. 1973. Nothing in biology makes sense except in the light of evolution. *The American biology teacher* 35(3). 125–129.

Dumas, Guillaume, Simon Malesys & Thomas Bourgeron. 2021. Systematic detection of brain protein-coding genes under positive selection during primate evolution and their roles in cognition. *Genome Research* 31(3). 484–496.

Eichert, Nicole, Lennart Verhagen, Davide Folloni, Saad Jbabdi, Alexandre A. Khrapitchev, Nicola R. Sibson, Dante Mantini, Jerome Sallet & Rogier B. Mars. 2019. What is special about the human arcuate fasciculus? Lateralization, projections, and expansion. *Cortex* 118. 107–115.

Enard, Wolfgang, Sabine Gehre, Kurt Hammerschmidt, Sabine M. Hölter, Torsten Blass, Mehmet Somel, Martina K. Brückner, Christiane Schreiweis, Christine Winter, Reinhard Sohr, et al. 2009. A humanized version of Foxp2 affects cortico-basal ganglia circuits in mice. *Cell* 137(5). 961–971.

Enard, Wolfgang, Molly Przeworski, Simon E. Fisher, Cecilia SL Lai, Victor Wiebe, Takashi Kitano, Anthony P. Monaco & Svante Pääbo. 2002. Molecular evolution of FOXP2, a gene involved in speech and language. *Nature* 418(6900). 869–872.

Everett, Caleb, Damián E. Blasi & Seán G. Roberts. 2015. Climate, vocal folds, and tonal languages: Connecting the physiological and geographic dots. *Proceedings of the National Academy of Sciences* 112(5). 1322–1327.

Fisher, Simon E. 2014. Translating the genome in human neuroscience. In Gary Marcus & Jeremy Freeman (eds.), *The future of the brain*, 149–158. Princeton: Princeton University Press.

Fisher, Simon E. 2019. Human genetics: The evolving story of FOXP2. *Current Biology* 29(2). R65–R67.

Fisher, Simon E. & Constance Scharff. 2009. FOXP2 as a molecular window into speech and language. *Trends in Genetics* 25(4). 166–177.

Fisher, Simon E. & Sonja C. Vernes. 2015. Genetics and the language sciences. *Annu. Rev. Linguist.* 1(1). 289–310.

Fitch, W. Tecumseh. 2010. *The evolution of language*. Cambridge: Cambridge University Press.

Fitch, W. Tecumseh. 2011. Unity and diversity in human language. *Philosophical Transactions of the Royal Society B: Biological Sciences* 366(1563). 376–388.

Fitch, W. Tecumseh. 2014. Toward a computational framework for cognitive biology: Unifying approaches from cognitive neuroscience and comparative cognition. *Physics of life reviews* 11(3). 329–364.

Fitch, W. Tecumseh. 2018a. Bio-linguistics: Monkeys break through the syntax barrier. *Current Biology* 28(12). R695–R697.

Fitch, W. Tecumseh. 2018b. What animals can teach us about human language: The phonological continuity hypothesis. *Current opinion in behavioral sciences* 21. 68–75.

Fitch, W. Tecumseh, Marc D. Hauser & Noam Chomsky. 2005. The evolution of the language faculty: Clarifications and implications. *Cognition* 97(2). 179–210.

Fitch, W. Tecumseh, Ludwig Huber & Thomas Bugnyar. 2010. Social cognition and the evolution of language: Constructing cognitive phylogenies. *Neuron* 65(6). 795–814.

Florio, Marta, Michael Heide, Anneline Pinson, Holger Brandl, Mareike Albert, Sylke Winkler, Pauline Wimberger, Wieland B. Huttner & Michael Hiller. 2018. Evolution and cell-type specificity of human-specific genes preferentially expressed in progenitors of fetal neocortex. *Elife* 7. e32332.

Fodor, Jerry A. 1983. *The modularity of mind.* Cambridge, Mass.: MIT press.

Friederici, Angela D. 2017. *Language in our brain: The origins of a uniquely human capacity.* Cambridge, Mass.: MIT Press.

Fujita, Koji. 2016. On certain fallacies in evolutionary linguistics and how one can eliminate them. In Koji Fujita & Cedric Boeckx (eds.), *Advances in biolinguistics: The human language faculty and its biological basis*, 141–152. New York: Routledge.

Gallistel, Charles R. 2009. The foundational abstractions. In Massimo Piattelli-Palmarini, Juan Uriagereka & Pello Salaburu (eds.), *Of minds and language*, 58–73. Oxford: Oxford University Press.

Gervain, Judit & Jacques Mehler. 2010. Speech perception and language acquisition in the first year of life. *Annual review of psychology* 61. 191–218.

Giandomenico, Stefano L. & Madeline A. Lancaster. 2017. Probing human brain evolution and development in organoids. *Current opinion in cell biology* 44. 36–43.

Girard-Buttoz, Cedric, Emiliano Zaccarella, Tatiana Bortolato, Angela D. Friederici, Roman M. Wittig & Catherine Crockford. 2021. Chimpanzees use numerous flexible vocal sequences with more than two vocal units: A step towards language? *bioRxiv*. 2021.02.03.429517.

Godinho, Ricardo Miguel, Penny Spikins & Paul O'Higgins. 2018. Supraorbital morphology and social dynamics in human evolution. *Nature ecology & evolution* 2(6). 956–961.

Graf, Thomas. 2014a. Beyond the apparent: Cognitive parallels between syntax and phonology. In Carson T. Schütze & Linnaea Stockall (eds.), *Connectedness: Papers by and for Sarah van Wagenen*, vol. 18 (UCLA Working Papers in Linguistics), 161–174.

Graf, Thomas. 2014b. *Dependencies in syntax and phonology: A computational comparison*. Slides of a talk given at NECPHON 2014, November 15, NYU, New York, New York.

Graf, Thomas. 2020. *Curbing feature coding: Strictly local feature assignment*. Slides of a talk given at *SCiL 2020*, January 2–5, co-located with the LSA 2020.

Green, Richard E., Johannes Krause, Adrian W. Briggs, Tomislav Maricic, Udo Stenzel, Martin Kircher, Nick Patterson, Heng Li, Weiwei Zhai, Markus Hsi-Yang Fritz, et al. 2010. A draft sequence of the Neandertal genome. *sScience* 328(5979). 710–722.

Gunz, Philipp, Simon Neubauer, Bruno Maureille & Jean-Jacques Hublin. 2010. Brain development after birth differs between Neanderthals and modern humans. *Current biology* 20(21). R921–R922.

Gunz, Philipp, Amanda K. Tilot, Katharina Wittfeld, Alexander Teumer, Chin Yang Shapland, Theo GM Van Erp, Michael Dannemann, Benjamin Vernot, Simon Neubauer, Tulio Guadalupe, et al. 2019. Neandertal introgression sheds light on modern human endocranial globularity. *Current Biology* 29(1). 120–127.

Gutiérrez-Ibáñez, Cristián, Andrew N. Iwaniuk & Douglas R. Wylie. 2018. Parrots have evolved a primate-like telencephalic-midbrain-cerebellar circuit. *Scientific reports* 8(1). 1–11.

Hagoort, Peter. 2018. Prerequisites for an evolutionary stance on the neurobiology of language. *Current opinion in behavioral sciences* 21. 191–194.

Hare, Brian. 2017. Survival of the friendliest: Homo sapiens evolved via selection for prosociality. *Annual review of psychology* 68. 155–186.

Haremaki, Tomomi, Jakob J. Metzger, Tiago Rito, M. Zeeshan Ozair, Fred Etoc & Ali H. Brivanlou. 2019. Self-organizing neuruloids model developmental aspects of huntington's disease in the ectodermal compartment. *Nature biotechnology* 37(10). 1198–1208.

Hauser, Marc D., Noam Chomsky & W. Tecumseh Fitch. 2002. The faculty of language: What is it, who has it, and how did it evolve? *Science* 298(5598). 1569–1579.

Hauser, Marc D., Charles Yang, Robert C. Berwick, Ian Tattersall, Michael J. Ryan, Jeffrey Watumull, Noam Chomsky & Richard C. Lewontin. 2014. The mystery of language evolution. *Frontiers in psychology* 5. 401.

Heide, Michael, Wieland B. Huttner & Felipe Mora-Bermúdez. 2018. Brain organoids as models to study human neocortex development and evolution. *Current opinion in cell biology* 55. 8–16.

Heine, Bernd & Tania Kuteva. 2002. On the evolution of grammatical forms. In Alison Wray (ed.), *The transition to language*, 376–398. Oxford: Oxford University Press.

Heinz, Jeffrey. 2018. The computational nature of phonological generalizations. In Larry Hyman & Frans Plank (eds.), *Phonological typology*, 126–195. Berlin: Mouton/de Gruyter.

Heinz, Jeffrey & William Idsardi. 2011. Sentence and word complexity. *Science* 333(6040). 295–297.

Hockett, C. 1960. The origin of speech. *Scientific American* 203(3). 88–97.

Hoeksema, Nienke, Laura Verga, Janine Mengede, Corné van Roessel, Stella Villanueva, Anna Salazar-Casals, Ana Rubio-Garcia, Branislava Ćurčić-Blake, Sonja C. Vernes & Andrea Ravignani. 2021. Neuroanatomy of the grey seal brain: Bringing pinnipeds into the neurobiological study of vocal learning. *Philosophical Transactions of the Royal Society B: Biological Sciences* 376(1836). 20200252.

Hublin, Jean-Jacques, Abdelouahed Ben-Ncer, Shara E. Bailey, Sarah E. Freidline, Simon Neubauer, Matthew M. Skinner, Inga Bergmann, Adeline Le Cabec, Stefano Benazzi, Katerina Harvati, et al. 2017. New fossils from Jebel Irhoud, Morocco and the pan-African origin of Homo sapiens. *Nature* 546(7657). 289–292.

Hublin, Jean-Jacques, Simon Neubauer & Philipp Gunz. 2015. Brain ontogeny and life history in Pleistocene hominins. *Philosophical Transactions of the Royal Society B: Biological Sciences* 370(1663). 20140062.

Huch, Meritxell, Juergen A. Knoblich, Matthias P. Lutolf & Alfonso Martinez-Arias. 2017. The hope and the hype of organoid research. *Development* 144(6). 938–941.

Hurford, James R. 1990. Nativist and functional explanations in language acquisition. *Logical issues in language acquisition* 85. 136.

Hurford, James R. 2007. *The origins of meaning: Language in the light of evolution*. Vol. 1. Oxford: Oxford University Press.

Irurtzun, Aritz. 2015. The "Globularization Hypothesis" of the language-ready brain as a developmental frame for prosodic bootstrapping theories of language acquisition. *Frontiers in psychology* 6. 1817.

Jackendoff, Ray. 1999. Possible stages in the evolution of the language capacity. *Trends in cognitive sciences* 3(7). 272–279.

Jackendoff, Ray. 2006. *How did language begin?* https://ase.tufts.edu/cogstud/jackendoff/papers/howdidlanguagebegin.pdf (20 September, 2021).

Jackendoff, Ray. 2010. Your theory of language evolution depends on your theory of language. In Richard K. Larson, Viviane Deprez & Hiroko Yamakido (eds.), *The evolution of human language: Biolinguistic perspectives*, 63–72. Cambridge: Cambridge University Press.

Jackendoff, Ray & Steven Pinker. 2005. The nature of the language faculty and its implications for evolution of language (Reply to Fitch, Hauser, and Chomsky). *Cognition* 97(2). 211–225.

Jarrett, Ben J. M. & Rebecca M. Kilner. 2018. "why" and "how" behavior evolves: A comment on Bailey et al. *Behavioral Ecology* 29(1). 15–16.

Jarvis, Erich D. 2019. Evolution of vocal learning and spoken language. *Science* 366(6461). 50–54.

Jiang, Xinjian, Tenghai Long, Weicong Cao, Junru Li, Stanislas Dehaene & Liping Wang. 2018. Production of supra-regular spatial sequences by macaque monkeys. *Current Biology* 28(12). 1851–1859.

Johnsson, Martin, Rie Henriksen & Dominic Wright. 2021. The neural crest cell hypothesis: No unified explanation for domestication. *Genetics* 219(1). iyab097.

Joshi, Aravind K. 1985. Tree adjoining grammars: How much context-sensitivity is required to provide reasonable structural descriptions? In David Dowty, Lauri Karttunen & Arnold Zwicky (eds.), *Natural language parsing*, 206–250. Cambridge: Cambridge University Press.

Kanton, Sabina, Michael James Boyle, Zhisong He, Malgorzata Santel, Anne Weigert, Fátima Sanchís-Calleja, Patricia Guijarro, Leila Sidow, Jonas Simon Fleck, Dingding Han, et al. 2019. Organoid single-cell genomic atlas uncovers human-specific features of brain development. *Nature* 574(7778). 418–422.

Karttunen, Lauri. 1993. Finite-state constraints. *The last phonological rule* 6. 173–194.

Kirby, Simon. 2001. Spontaneous evolution of linguistic structure-an iterated learning model of the emergence of regularity and irregularity. *IEEE Transactions on Evolutionary Computation* 5(2). 102–110.

Kirby, Simon. 2017. Culture and biology in the origins of linguistic structure. *Psychonomic bulletin & review* 24(1). 118–137.

Kirby, Simon, Hannah Cornish & Kenny Smith. 2008. Cumulative cultural evolution in the laboratory: An experimental approach to the origins of structure in human language. *Proceedings of the National Academy of Sciences* 105(31). 10681–10686.

Kirby, Simon, Monica Tamariz, Hannah Cornish & Kenny Smith. 2015. Compression and communication in the cultural evolution of linguistic structure. *Cognition* 141. 87–102.

Kochiyama, Takanori, Naomichi Ogihara, Hiroki C. Tanabe, Osamu Kondo, Hideki Amano, Kunihiro Hasegawa, Hiromasa Suzuki, Marcia S. Ponce De León, Christoph PE Zollikofer, Markus Bastir, et al. 2018. Reconstructing the Neanderthal brain using computational anatomy. *Scientific reports* 8(1). 1–9.

Krakauer, John W., Asif A. Ghazanfar, Alex Gomez-Marin, Malcolm A. MacIver & David Poeppel. 2017. Neuroscience needs behavior: Correcting a reductionist bias. *Neuron* 93(3). 480–490.

Krupenye, Christopher & Josep Call. 2019. Theory of mind in animals: Current and future directions. *Wiley Interdisciplinary Reviews: Cognitive Science* 10(6). e1503.

Kuhlwilm, Martin & Cedric Boeckx. 2019. A catalog of single nucleotide changes distinguishing modern humans from archaic hominins. *Scientific reports* 9(1). 1–14.

Lai, Cecilia S. L., Simon E. Fisher, Jane A. Hurst, Faraneh Vargha-Khadem & Anthony P. Monaco. 2001. A forkhead-domain gene is mutated in a severe speech and language disorder. *Nature* 413(6855). 519–523.

Lambert, D., J. Rawski & J. Heinz. 2021. Typology emerges from simplicity in representations and learning. *Journal of Language Modelling* 9. 1.

Lameira, Adriano R. 2017. Bidding evidence for primate vocal learning and the cultural substrates for speech evolution. *Neuroscience & Biobehavioral Reviews* 83. 429–439.

Lancaster, Madeline A., Magdalena Renner, Carol-Anne Martin, Daniel Wenzel, Louise S. Bicknell, Matthew E. Hurles, Tessa Homfray, Josef M. Penninger, Andrew P. Jackson & Juergen A. Knoblich. 2013. Cerebral organoids model human brain development and microcephaly. *Nature* 501(7467). 373–379.

Lasnik, Howard. 2000. *Syntactic structures revisited: Contemporary lectures on classic transformational theory*. Vol. 33. Cambridge, Mass.: MIT Press.

Lattenkamp, Ella Z. & Sonja C. Vernes. 2018. Vocal learning: A language-relevant trait in need of a broad cross-species approach. *Current opinion in behavioral sciences* 21. 209–215.

Lenneberg, EH. 1967. *Biological foundations of language*. New York: Wiley.

Lewontin, Richard C. 1998. The evolution of cognition: Questions we will never answer. *An invitation to cognitive science* 4. 107–132.

Lewontin, Richard C. 2001. *The triple helix: Gene, organism, and environment*. Cambridge, Mass.: Harvard University Press.

Linz, David M., Yonggang Hu & Armin P. Moczek. 2019. The origins of novelty from within the confines of homology: The developmental evolution of the digging tibia of dung beetles. *Proceedings of the Royal Society B*. 286(1896). 20182427.

Lord, Kathryn A., Greger Larson, Raymond P. Coppinger & Elinor K. Karlsson. 2020. The history of farm foxes undermines the animal domestication syndrome. *Trends in ecology & evolution* 35(2). 125–136.

Mafessoni, Fabrizio, Steffi Grote, Cesare de Filippo, Viviane Slon, Kseniya A. Kolobova, Bence Viola, Sergey V. Markin, Manjusha Chintalapati, Stephane Peyrégne, Laurits Skov, et al. 2020. A high-coverage Neandertal genome from Chagyrskaya Cave. *Proceedings of the National Academy of Sciences* 117(26). 15132–15136.

Malassis, Raphaëlle, Stanislas Dehaene & Joël Fagot. 2020. Baboons (Papio papio) process a context-free but not a context-sensitive grammar. *Scientific reports* 10(1). 1–12.

Marantz, Alec. 2019. *What do linguists do?* Ms., NYU.

Marcus, Gary. 2009. *Kluge: The haphazard evolution of the human mind.* New York: Houghton Mifflin Harcourt.

Marr, David. 1982. *Vision: A computational investigation into the human representation and processing of visual information.* San Francisco: W. H. Freeman.

Martins, Pedro Tiago & Cedric Boeckx. 2016. What we talk about when we talk about biolinguistics. *Linguistics Vanguard* 2(1). 20160007.

Martins, Pedro Tiago & Cedric Boeckx. 2019. Language evolution and complexity considerations: The no half-merge fallacy. *PLoS biology* 17(11). e3000389.

Martins, Pedro Tiago & Cedric Boeckx. 2020a. Clarifications on the no half-Merge fallacy. *Lingbuzz*. 005432.

Martins, Pedro Tiago & Cedric Boeckx. 2020b. Vocal learning: Beyond the continuum. *PLoS biology* 18(3). e3000672.

Mayr, Ernst. 2000. Darwin's influence on modern thought. *Scientific American* 283(1). 78–83.

McCauley, Stewart M. & Morten H. Christiansen. 2019. Language learning as language use: A cross-linguistic model of child language development. *Psychological review* 126(1). 1.

Meader, Clarence L. & John H. Muyskens. 1950. *Handbook of biolinguistics.* Toledo: H. C. Weller.

Mendívil Giró, José Luis. 2019. Did language evolve through language change? On language change, language evolution and grammaticalization theory. *Glossa* 4(1). 124.

Meyer, Matthias, Martin Kircher, Marie-Theres Gansauge, Heng Li, Fernando Racimo, Swapan Mallick, Joshua G. Schraiber, Flora Jay, Kay Prüfer, Cesare De Filippo, et al. 2012. A high-coverage genome sequence from an archaic Denisovan individual. *Science* 338(6104). 222–226.

Mitchell, Kevin J. 2018. *Innate.* Princeton: Princeton University Press.

Miura, Yuki, Min-Yin Li, Fikri Birey, Kazuya Ikeda, Omer Revah, Mayuri Vijay Thete, Jin-Young Park, Alyssa Puno, Samuel H. Lee, Matthew H. Porteus, et al. 2020. Generation of human striatal organoids and cortico-striatal assembloids from human pluripotent stem cells. *Nature Biotechnology* 38(12). 1421–1430.

Moczek, Armin P. 2008. On the origins of novelty in development and evolution. *BioEssays* 30(5). 432–447.

Moore, Richard. 2018a. Gricean communication, joint action, and the evolution of cooperation. *Topoi* 37(2). 329–341.

Moore, Richard. 2018b. Gricean communication, language development, and animal minds. *Philosophy Compass* 13(12). e12550.

Mora-Bermúdez, Felipe, Farhath Badsha, Sabina Kanton, J. Gray Camp, Benjamin Vernot, Kathrin Köhler, Birger Voigt, Keisuke Okita, Tomislav Maricic, Zhisong He, et al. 2016. Differences and similarities between human and chimpanzee neural progenitors during cerebral cortex development. *Elife* 5. e18683.

Motamedi, Yasamin, Marieke Schouwstra, Kenny Smith, Jennifer Culbertson & Simon Kirby. 2019. Evolving artificial sign languages in the lab: From improvised gesture to systematic sign. *Cognition* 192. 103964.

Muchnik, Sydney Keaton, Belen Lorente-Galdos, Gabriel Santpere & Nenad Sestan. 2019. Modeling the evolution of human brain development using organoids. *Cell* 179(6). 1250–1253.

Müller, Gerd B. & Stuart A. Newman. 2005. The innovation triad: An EvoDevo agenda. *Journal of Experimental Zoology Part B: Molecular and Developmental Evolution* 304(6). 487–503.

Müller, Gerd B. & Gunter P. Wagner. 1991. Novelty in evolution: Restructuring the concept. *Annual review of ecology and systematics* 22(1). 229–256.

Neubauer, Simon, Jean-Jacques Hublin & Philipp Gunz. 2018. The evolution of modern human brain shape. *Science advances* 4(1). eaao5961.

O'Donnell, Timothy J., Marc D. Hauser & W. Tecumseh Fitch. 2005. Using mathematical models of language experimentally. *Trends in Cognitive Sciences* 9(6). 284–289.

O'Rourke, Thomas, Pedro Tiago Martins, Rie Asano, Ryosuke O. Tachibana, Kazuo Okanoya & Cedric Boeckx. 2021. Capturing the effects of domestication on vocal learning complexity. *Trends in cognitive sciences* 25(6). 462–474.

O'Rourke, Thomas & Cedric Boeckx. 2020. Glutamate receptors in domestication and modern human evolution. *Neuroscience & Biobehavioral Reviews* 108. 341–357.

Okanoya, Kazuo. 2004. The Bengalese finch: A window on the behavioral neurobiology of birdsong syntax. *Annals of the New York Academy of Sciences* 1016(1). 724–735.

Okanoya, Kazuo. 2017. Sexual communication and domestication may give rise to the signal complexity necessary for the emergence of language: An indication from songbird studies. *Psychonomic bulletin & review* 24(1). 106–110.

Orpella, Joan, Pablo Ripollés, Manuela Ruzzoli, Julià L. Amengual, Alicia Callejas, Anna Martinez-Alvarez, Salvador Soto-Faraco & Ruth de Diego-Balaguer. 2020. Integrating when and what information in the left parietal lobe allows language rule generalization. *PLoS biology* 18(11). e3000895.

Pääbo, Svante. 2014a. *Neanderthal man: In search of lost genomes.* London: Hachette UK.

Pääbo, Svante. 2014b. The human condition: A molecular approach. *Cell* 157(1). 216–226.

Pereira-Pedro, Ana Sofia, Emiliano Bruner, Philipp Gunz & Simon Neubauer. 2020. A morphometric comparison of the parietal lobe in modern humans and Neanderthals. *Journal of human evolution* 142. 102770.

Petkov, Christopher I. & Erich D. Jarvis. 2012. Birds, primates, and spoken language origins: Behavioral phenotypes and neurobiological substrates. *Frontiers in evolutionary neuroscience* 4. 12.

Petkov, Christopher I. & Benjamin Wilson. 2012. On the pursuit of the brain network for proto-syntactic learning in non-human primates: Conceptual issues and neurobiological hypotheses. *Philosophical Transactions of the Royal Society B: Biological Sciences* 367(1598). 2077–2088.

Pfenning, Andreas R., Erina Hara, Osceola Whitney, Miriam V. Rivas, Rui Wang, Petra L. Roulhac, Jason T. Howard, Morgan Wirthlin, Peter V. Lovell, Ganeshkumar Ganapathy, et al. 2014. Convergent transcriptional specializations in the brains of humans and song-learning birds. *Science* 346(6215). 1256846.

Piattelli-Palmarini, Massimo & Juan Uriagereka. 2011. A geneticist's dream, a linguist's nightmare: The case of FOXP2. In Anna-Maria Di Sciullo & Cedric Boeckx (eds.), *The biolinguistic enterprise*, 101–125. Oxford: Oxford University Press.

Pidoux, Ludivine, Pascale Le Blanc, Carole Levenes & Arthur Leblois. 2018. A subcortical circuit linking the cerebellum to the basal ganglia engaged in vocal learning. *Elife* 7. e32167.

Pinker, Steven & Ray Jackendoff. 2005. The faculty of language: What's special about it? *Cognition* 95(2). 201–236.

Pleyer, Michael & Stefan Hartmann. 2020. Construction grammar for monkeys?: Animal communication and its implications for language evolution in the light of usage-based linguistic theory. *Evolutionary Linguistic Theory* 2(2). 153–194.

Poeppel, David. 2012. The maps problem and the mapping problem: Two challenges for a cognitive neuroscience of speech and language. *Cognitive neuropsychology* 29(1-2). 34–55.

Poeppel, David & David Embick. 2005. Defining the relation between linguistics and neuroscience. *Twenty-first century psycholinguistics: Four cornerstones* 1. 103–118.

Pollen, Alex A., Aparna Bhaduri, Madeline G. Andrews, Tomasz J. Nowakowski, Olivia S. Meyerson, Mohammed A. Mostajo-Radji, Elizabeth Di Lullo, Beatriz Alvarado, Melanie Bedolli, Max L. Dougherty, Ian T. Fiddes, Zev N. Kronenberg, Joe Shuga, Anne A. Leyrat, Jay A. West, Marina Bershteyn, Craig B. Lowe, Bryan J. Pavlovic, Sofie R. Salama, David Haussler, Evan E. Eichler & Arnold R. Kriegstein. 2019. Establishing cerebral organoids as models of human-specific brain evolution. *Cell* 176(4). 743–756.

Progovac, Ljiljana. 2015. *Evolutionary syntax*. Vol. 20. Oxford: Oxford University Press.

Prud'homme, Benjamin, Caroline Minervino, Mélanie Hocine, Jessica D. Cande, Aïcha Aouane, Héloïse D. Dufour, Victoria A. Kassner & Nicolas Gompel. 2011. Body plan innovation in treehoppers through the evolution of an extra winglike appendage. *Nature* 473(7345). 83–86.

Prüfer, Kay, Cesare de Filippo, Steffi Grote, Fabrizio Mafessoni, Petra Korlević, Mateja Hajdinjak, Benjamin Vernot, Laurits Skov, Pinghsun Hsieh, Stéphane Peyrégne, et al. 2017. A high-coverage Neandertal genome from Vindija Cave in Croatia. *Science* 358(6363). 655–658.

Prüfer, Kay, Fernando Racimo, Nick Patterson, Flora Jay, Sriram Sankararaman, Susanna Sawyer, Anja Heinze, Gabriel Renaud, Peter H. Sudmant, Cesare De Filippo, et al. 2014. The complete genome sequence of a Neanderthal from the Altai Mountains. *Nature* 505(7481). 43–49.

Raviv, Limor. 2020. *Language and society: How social pressures shape grammatical structure*. Radboud University Nijmegen Nijmegen. (Doctoral dissertation).

Raviv, Limor, Marianne de Heer Kloots & Antje Meyer. 2021. What makes a language easy to learn? A preregistered study on how systematic structure and community size affect language learnability. *Cognition* 210. 104620.

Raviv, Limor, Antje Meyer & Shiri Lev-Ari. 2019. Larger communities create more systematic languages. *Proceedings of the Royal Society B* 286(1907). 20191262.

Reich, David. 2018. *Who we are and how we got here: Ancient DNA and the new science of the human past*. Oxford: Oxford University Press.

Rilling, James K., Matthew F. Glasser, Todd M. Preuss, Xiangyang Ma, Tiejun Zhao, Xiaoping Hu & Timothy E. J. Behrens. 2008. The evolution of the arcuate fasciculus revealed with comparative DTI. *Nature neuroscience* 11(4). 426–428.

Rogers, James & Geoffrey K. Pullum. 2011. Aural pattern recognition experiments and the subregular hierarchy. *Journal of Logic, Language and Information* 20(3). 329–342.

Samuels, Bridget D. 2011. *Phonological architecture: A biolinguistic perspective*. Vol. 2. Oxford: Oxford University Press.

Samuels, Bridget D. 2015. Can a bird brain do phonology? *Frontiers in psychology* 6. 1082.

Scerri, Eleanor M. L., Mark G. Thomas, Andrea Manica, Philipp Gunz, Jay T. Stock, Chris Stringer, Matt Grove, Huw S. Groucutt, Axel Timmermann, G. Philip Rightmire, et al. 2018. Did our species evolve in subdivided populations across Africa, and why does it matter? *Trends in ecology & evolution* 33(8). 582–594.

Schlenker, Philippe, Emmanuel Chemla, Anne M. Schel, James Fuller, Jean-Pierre Gautier, Jeremy Kuhn, Dunja Veselinović, Kate Arnold, Cristiane Cäsar, Sumir Keenan, et al. 2016. Formal monkey linguistics. *Theoretical Linguistics* 42(1-2). 1–90.

Scott-Phillips, Thomas C. & Simon Kirby. 2010. Language evolution in the laboratory. *Trends in cognitive sciences* 14(9). 411–417.

Slon, Viviane, Charlotte Hopfe, Clemens L. Weiß, Fabrizio Mafessoni, Marco De La Rasilla, Carles Lalueza-Fox, Antonio Rosas, Marie Soressi, Monika V. Knul, Rebecca Miller, et al. 2017. Neandertal and denisovan DNA from pleistocene sediments. *Science* 356(6338). 605–608.

Smolensky, Paul & Alan Prince. 2004. *Optimality Theory: Constraint interaction in generative grammar*. New York: Wiley.

Stabler, Edward P. 2011. Computational perspectives on minimalism. In Cedric Boeckx (ed.), *Oxford handbook of linguistic minimalism*, 617–643. Oxford: Oxford University Press.

Stabler, Edward P. 2013. The epicenter of linguistic behavior. In Montserrat Sanz, Itziar Laka & Michael K. Tanenhaus (eds.), *Language down the garden path: The cognitive and biological basis of linguistic structures*, 316–323. Oxford: Oxford University Press.

Straub, Isabelle, Laurens Witter, Abdelmoneim Eshra, Miriam Hoidis, Niklas Byczkowicz, Sebastian Maas, Igor Delvendahl, Kevin Dorgans, Elise Savier, Ingo Bechmann, et al. 2020. Gradients in the mammalian cerebellar cortex enable Fourier-like transformation and improve storing capacity. *Elife* 9. e51771.

Stringer, Chris. 2016. The origin and evolution of Homo sapiens. *Philosophical Transactions of the Royal Society B: Biological Sciences* 371(1698). 20150237.

Theofanopoulou, Constantina & Cedric Boeckx. 2015. Cognitive phylogenies, the Darwinian logic of descent, and the inadequacy of cladistic thinking. *Frontiers in Cell and Developmental Biology* 3. 64.

Theofanopoulou, Constantina, Cedric Boeckx & Erich D. Jarvis. 2017. A hypothesis on a role of oxytocin in the social mechanisms of speech and vocal learning. *Proceedings of the Royal Society B: Biological Sciences* 284(1861). 20170988.

Theofanopoulou, Constantina, Simone Gastaldon, Thomas O'Rourke, Bridget D. Samuels, Pedro Tiago Martins, Francesco Delogu, Saleh Alamri & Cedric Boeckx. 2017. Self-domestication in homo sapiens: Insights from comparative genomics. *PloS one* 12(10). e0185306.

Thomas, James. 2014. *Self-domestication and language evolution*. The University of Edinburgh. (Doctoral dissertation).

Thomas, James & Simon Kirby. 2018. Self domestication and the evolution of language. *Biology & philosophy* 33(1). 1–30.

Thompson, Bill, Simon Kirby & Kenny Smith. 2016. Culture shapes the evolution of cognition. *Proceedings of the National Academy of Sciences* 113(16). 4530–4535.

Tinbergen, Niko. 1963. On aims and methods of ethology. *Zeitschrift für Tierpsychologie* 20(4). 410–433.

Trujillo, Cleber A., Edward S. Rice, Nathan K. Schaefer, Isaac A. Chaim, Emily C. Wheeler, Assael A. Madrigal, Justin Buchanan, Sebastian Preissl, Allen Wang, Priscilla D. Negraes, Ryan A. Szeto, Roberto H. Herai, Alik Huseynov, Mariana S. A. Ferraz, Fernando S. Borges, Alexandre H. Kihara, Ashley Byrne, Maximillian Marin, Christopher Vollmers, Angela N. Brooks, Jonathan D. Lautz, Katerina Semendeferi, Beth Shapiro, Gene W. Yeo, Stephen E. P. Smith, Richard E. Green & Alysson R. Muotri. 2021. Reintroduction of the archaic variant of NOVA1 in cortical organoids alters neurodevelopment. *Science* 371(6530).

Uriagereka, Juan. 2008. *Syntactic anchors: On semantic structuring*. Cambridge: Cambridge University Press.

Verhoef, Tessa, Simon Kirby & Bart de Boer. 2013. Combinatorial structure and iconicity in artificial whistled languages. In *Proceedings of the annual meeting of the cognitive science society*, vol. 35.

Vernot, Benjamin, Elena I. Zavala, Asier Gómez-Olivencia, Zenobia Jacobs, Viviane Slon, Fabrizio Mafessoni, Frédéric Romagné, Alice Pearson, Martin Petr, Nohemi Sala, et al. 2021. Unearthing Neanderthal population history using nuclear and mitochondrial DNA from cave sediments. *Science* 372(6542). eabf1667.

Watson, Stuart K., Judith M. Burkart, Steven J. Schapiro, Susan P. Lambeth, Jutta L. Mueller & Simon W. Townsend. 2020. Nonadjacent dependency processing in monkeys, apes, and humans. *Science advances* 6(43). eabb0725.

Weiss, Carly V., Lana Harshman, Fumitaka Inoue, Hunter B. Fraser, Dmitri A. Petrov, Nadav Ahituv & David Gokhman. 2021. The cis-regulatory effects of modern human-specific variants. *Elife* 10. e63713.

Welker, Frido, Mateja Hajdinjak, Sahra Talamo, Klervia Jaouen, Michael Dannemann, Francine David, Michèle Julien, Matthias Meyer, Janet Kelso, Ian Barnes, et al. 2016. Palaeoproteomic evidence identifies archaic hominins associated with the Châtelperronian at the Grotte du Renne. *Proceedings of the National Academy of Sciences* 113(40). 11162–11167.

Welker, Frido, Jazmín Ramos-Madrigal, Petra Gutenbrunner, Meaghan Mackie, Shivani Tiwary, Rosa Rakownikow Jersie-Christensen, Cristina Chiva, Marc R. Dickinson, Martin Kuhlwilm, Marc de Manuel, et al. 2020. The dental proteome of homo antecessor. *Nature* 580(7802). 235–238.

Wilkins, Adam S., Richard Wrangham & W. Tecumseh Fitch. 2021. The neural crest/domestication syndrome hypothesis, explained: Reply to Johnsson, Henriksen, and Wright. *Genetics* 219(1).

Wilkins, Adam S., Richard W. Wrangham & W. Tecumseh Fitch. 2014. The "domestication syndrome" in mammals: A unified explanation based on neural crest cell behavior and genetics. *Genetics* 197(3). 795–808.

Wilson, Benjamin, William D. Marslen-Wilson & Christopher I. Petkov. 2017. Conserved sequence processing in primate frontal cortex. *Trends in neurosciences* 40(2). 72–82.

Wirthlin, Morgan, Edward F. Chang, Mirjam Knörnschild, Leah A. Krubitzer, Claudio V. Mello, Cory T. Miller, Andreas R. Pfenning, Sonja C. Vernes, Ofer Tchernichovski & Michael M. Yartsev. 2019. A modular approach to vocal learning: Disentangling the diversity of a complex behavioral trait. *Neuron* 104(1). 87–99.

Wirthlin, Morgan, Nicholas C. B. Lima, Rafael Lucas Muniz Guedes, André ER Soares, Luiz Gonzaga P. Almeida, Nathalia P. Cavaleiro, Guilherme Loss de Morais, Anderson V. Chaves, Jason T. Howard, Marcus de Melo Teixeira, et al. 2018. Parrot genomes and the evolution of heightened longevity and cognition. *Current Biology* 28(24). 4001–4008.

Wrangham, Richard W. 2018. Two types of aggression in human evolution. *Proceedings of the National Academy of Sciences* 115(2). 245–253.

Zanella, Matteo, Alessandro Vitriolo, Alejandro Andirko, Pedro Tiago Martins, Stefanie Sturm, Thomas O'Rourke, Magdalena Laugsch, Natascia Malerba, Adrianos Skaros, Sebastiano Trattaro, et al. 2019. Dosage analysis of the 7q11.

23 williams region identifies BAZ1B as a major human gene patterning the modern human face and underlying self-domestication. *Science advances* 5(12). eaaw7908.

Zavala, Elena I., Zenobia Jacobs, Benjamin Vernot, Michael V. Shunkov, Maxim B. Kozlikin, Anatoly P. Derevianko, Elena Essel, Cesare de Fillipo, Sarah Nagel, Julia Richter, et al. 2021. Pleistocene sediment DNA reveals hominin and faunal turnovers at denisova cave. *Nature* 595(7867). 399–403.

Name index